Agrarianism and Reconstruction Politics

MICHAEL L. LANZA

Agrarianism and Reconstruction Politics

The Southern Homestead Act

LOUISIANA STATE UNIVERSITY PRESS
Baton Rouge and London

Manufactured in the United States of America

First printing
99 98 97 96 95 94 93 92 91 90 5 4 3 2 1

DESIGNER:
Pat Crowder
TYPEFACE:
Linotron 202 Aster
TYPESETTER:
The Composing Room of Michigan, Inc.
PRINTER AND BINDER:
Thomson-Shore, Inc.

LIBRARY OF CONGRESS CATALOGING-IN-PUBLICATION DATA

Lanza, Michael L., 1953–
Agrarianism and Reconstruction politics : the Southern Homestead Act / Michael L. Lanza.
p. cm.
Bibliography: p.
Includes index.
ISBN 0-8071-1545-2 (alk. paper)
1. Homestead law—Southern States—History. I. Title.
KF5670.L36 1989
346.7504'32—dc20
[347.506432] 89-12137
CIP

The paper in this book meets the guidelines for permanence and durability of the Committee on Production Guidelines for Book Longevity of the Council on Library Resources. ♾

To my parents, Joe and Flo,
with much love

Contents

Acknowledgments

This project has been a long one, having been begun in the late 1970s. The manuscript has since been cut drastically and its direction refocused. Many people have contributed to this endeavor along the way, and I would like to express my heartfelt thanks to them by mentioning them here.

Staff members at several libraries were extremely helpful, particularly at the Georgetown Law School library and at the Library of Congress. People at the National Archives, especially those serving in 11E–2, were much too generous with their time and friendship for the three years I worked there. That room is no longer open because of budget cuts. I fear this project might never have been completed had I not had access to the valuable material firsthand. What happens when we no longer have ready access to our history? All the staff deserve thanks, but I would like to single out Darryl Munsey and James Rush, who continued to find documents for me long after I had left Washington.

I should also like to thank several librarians in Mississippi who helped me locate some Mississippi homesteaders for the statistical study. Some even went so far as to do the research for me, providing me with valuable information and making my own work easier. I am especially grateful to the following: Murella Hebert Powell of the Biloxi public library; Dorothy L. Cook of Attala County; Carol B. Bunch of the Waynesboro memorial library; Emily T. Cosby in Pascagoula; Marion Tillson in Smith County; Kathryn Ervin Stutts of

Forest; Margaret Yates of the Meridian public library; and Theresa Ridout of Neshoba County.

My colleagues at Virginia Tech, Middlebury College, and the University of New Orleans were always supportive and eager to have this work completed. A special note of thanks must go to the College of Liberal Arts at the University of New Orleans for a grant that allowed me to complete the statistical part of the book. I should also like to thank Joseph Logsdon and Jerah Johnson of UNO, who read parts of the manuscript and offered valuable suggestions.

I should also like to thank the courteous and professional staff at LSU Press for seeing this project through. Beverly Jarrett took an early interest in the manuscript and hounded me until I placed it in her hands. My copy editor, Joan Seward, was particularly meticulous and a pleasure to work with.

Much of this study would not have been possible without the assistance of Donald T. Gantz of George Mason University. He is a statistician *par excellence,* and his know-how and his patience seemed without limit. He convinced me that computers were worth learning and that they really could be useful tools and not ends in themselves. He was as excited about my Mississippi homesteaders as I was.

To John Hope Franklin, I owe more than any brief acknowledgment could ever convey. His example during my stay at Chicago, as well as his friendship, encouragement, and support, have been a great source of inspiration. His critical eye was always appreciated, and his interest in the project, even through publication, was unwavering. His example as historian and human being will be difficult to follow.

Friends and family have also been supportive. Mary Stovall of Brigham Young University offered me more encouragement than she knows. Joe Gray Taylor was an early teacher, and Lance Van Dyke pushed me hard when things seemed to cave in. And the dedication to my parents is a small token of my appreciation for everything they have done.

Despite all of these people, I must also take responsibility for any errors of fact or judgment in this work.

Abbreviations

Division "A," Letters Sent	Division "A," Letters Sent to Registers and Receivers of Local Land Offices. Record Group 49, National Archives, Washington, D.C.
GLO	General Land Office
Letters Sent	Division "C," Letters Sent to Registers and Receivers, Record Group 49
MLR	Division "D," Miscellaneous Letters Received from Private Persons, Land Entrymen, Attorneys, and Other Persons, Record Group 49
R&R	Register and Receiver
SG Letters Received	Division "E," Letters Received from Surveyors General, Record Group 49
SG Letters Sent	Division "E," Letters Sent to Surveyors General, Record Group 49

Agrarianism and Reconstruction Politics

Introduction

For centuries the abundance and cheapness of land drew settlers to America's shores, and thence across the continent. Ownership of land not only formed the foundation of the new democracy; it also became the key to its economic advancement. But not all Americans shared in that opportunity. Black Americans were denied the promise of property almost from the beginning. Either they were slaves, or courts and legislation cut them off from the American dream. With emancipation came the need to provide some economic base to freedmen, and the thoughts of policy makers turned naturally to land, the age-old solution. The result was the Southern Homestead Act of 1866, which promised federal lands to landless citizens, free of charge and without discrimination based on race.

This act, which opened the 46 million acres of federal lands in Alabama, Arkansas, Florida, Louisiana, and Mississippi, differed from previous homestead laws most significantly in that it restricted the southern lands solely to homesteading. Under its provisions, no one was allowed to purchase property directly; hence, speculators were cut out altogether and the lands were reserved strictly for the underprivileged. This restriction was the product of three closely related developments. First, the tenets of agrarianism had traditionally favored small farmers over corporations, speculators, and business interests. And second, the Republican party favored the ideal of "homestead-only" legislation because it fit with the free soil, free labor ideology it had developed in the 1850s. As this ideology matured during the Civil War, it came to include a third element, the notion of punishing or, at the very least, limiting any further aggrandizements of southern plantation owners who, most Republicans believed, were responsible for the rebellion.

The tenets of agrarianism dated back at least to the beginnings of the Republic. This philosophy, which called for the equitable distribution of America's vast abundance of land, made the yeoman farmer the bedrock of democracy and freedom. In 1776, Thomas Jefferson, one of the earliest spokesmen for agrarianism, called small farmers the true Americans, "the most precious part" of the nation. They represented the best hope for the country's future prosperity as well as the preservation of its democracy. And half a century later, Andrew Jackson echoed Jefferson in his 1832 State of the Union message to Congress: "Independent farmers are everywhere the basis of society and true friends of liberty."[1]

But Jackson also added something new. In the same speech, he called for the "speedy settlement" of the unoccupied public domain. That sounded a shift in U.S. public land policy. Up to that time, the government had viewed the sale of public lands as a source of revenue for the treasury. But Jackson moved the nation toward the idea that public lands should be sold cheaply and quickly in order to spread more rapidly the population over the whole country. When Congress passed the Preemption Act in 1841, it recognized for the first time settlers' rights to lands they had already occupied.

By the 1850s, the dispersal of the population became tied to the slavery issue. The new Republican party took up the theme of cheap, or even free, land for settlers from "the laboring classes," and linked it to their insistence that new territories should be kept free of slavery. As the debate over slavery in the territories heated up, various homesteading bills were introduced in Congress. In every case, the question of how black people would fare arose. Slaves, obviously, would be excluded. But would free blacks have a right to

1. Thomas Jefferson to Edmund Pendleton, August 13, 1776, in Julian Boyd (ed)., *The Papers of Thomas Jefferson* (Princeton, 1950), I, 492; Fred L. Israel (ed.), *The State of the Union Messages of the Presidents 1790–1966* (New York, 1966), I, 367.

claim land? When one measure came up for consideration in 1852, a congressman from Massachusetts urged that separate territory be set aside for Negroes so they would not settle among whites. In 1854, with another homestead measure pending, a Pennsylvania representative moved that the word *white* be inserted in the language of the bill so that no one would mistake the beneficiaries of the law. Several of his colleagues pointed out that such exclusions were unnecessary because states did not recognize Negroes as citizens anyway. But the amendment's sponsor argued that it was important to express plainly who could have land in order to raise the bill above judicial rulings on the matter. His amendment passed, though the bill, like its predecessors, ultimately failed.[2] The Supreme Court seemed to settle the issue with its 1857 Dred Scott ruling that Negroes held none of the rights of national citizenship. Hence, they could lay no claims to federal lands.

But secession, confiscation of federal lands by the states, and the war changed everything. In 1862, Congress succeeded in passing a Homestead Act that granted land free to any who would settle it. When Reconstruction began, however, that act proved inadequate to the needs of freedmen, for it made no reference to black Americans one way or another; it spoke only of "citizens." While North and South were still engaged in fighting, the federal government made several piecemeal attempts to provide former slaves with land. General Sherman's renting to freedmen abandoned lands on the Sea Islands of South Carolina and Georgia, and the distribution, in other parts of the South, of confiscated plantation lands to former slave tenants are well known.[3] Further, during Reconstruction the Freedmen's Bureau sought to help former slaves acquire land.

2. *Congressional Globe,* 32nd Cong., 1st Sess., 396; *Congressional Globe,* 33rd Cong., 1st Sess., 503–504. The vote on the amendment was 101 to 78 and is in the *House Journal,* 33rd Cong., 1st Sess., 456.

3. George R. Bentley, *A History of the Freedmen's Bureau* (Philadelphia, 1955); LaWanda Cox, "The Promise of Land for the Freedmen," *Mississippi Valley Historical Review,* XLV (1958), 413–40; Claude F. Oubre, "The Freedmen's Bureau and Negro Land Ownership" (M.A. thesis, University of Southwestern Louisiana, 1970); Claude F. Oubre, *Forty Acres and a Mule* (Baton Rouge, 1978); Willie Lee Rose, *Rehearsal for Reconstruction: The Port Royal Experiment* (London, 1964).

Not until passage of the Southern Homestead Act in 1866 was a full-scale solution attempted. That act opened federal lands in the southern states to homesteading and specified that applicants could not be discriminated against on the basis of color. It was a grand visionary attempt to legislatively right old wrongs, reorient the South's economy to bring it more into conformity with the rest of the country, and inaugurate a massive social reform by providing a newly freed citizenry with an economic base for their future advancement.

Although some people got land, the act failed—at least so far as the intentions of the framers were concerned—and was repealed after only ten years. Part of the story of its failure was the poor quality of the public lands themselves; part the bureaucratic entanglements in the General Land Office in Washington and in local offices. Part was the quality of political appointees administering the program; part the opposition of white southern landowners. Part of the story was increasing Republican concern with attracting the support of southern conservatives for their economic program; part a consequent shrinking of the original commitment to the ideal of equal rights for freedmen. And part was a new emphasis on the economic development of the South, development of a sort that required close cooperation of eastern and southern establishment interests.

The Southern Homestead Act failed in its framers' intent of providing freedmen with a viable economic base. Its history can tell us much about the Republicans' inability to extend the Jeffersonian dream of small farms to black southerners as well as the new reality of a modern industrializing America not anticipated by the assumptions and myths associated with an earlier rural frontier.

I

In the Halls of Congress

When Andrew Johnson signed the Southern Homestead Act on June 21, 1866, it took its place among some of the most important legislation passed during the "critical year," including the Civil Rights Act and the Fourteenth Amendment. The measure, for the first six months after passage, opened the federal public lands in the South to settlement by only freedmen and whites loyal to the Union. Then, after the first of the year, anyone who met the minimum age and citizenship requirements could apply. A supplement to the Homestead Act of 1862, it significantly extended existing American public land policy by specifically restricting the southern public lands to homestead settlement only. For the first time in American history, lawmakers had devised legislation based solely on the principles of agrarianism.

The tenets of agrarianism dated back to Thomas Jefferson, who believed and forcefully proclaimed that small farmers who owned and worked their own lands made the best citizens in a republic. Like other enlightened figures of his day, Jefferson believed that a person had a natural right to private property, and ownership of land went hand in hand with other rights such as "life, liberty, and the pursuit of happiness." America's abundance had already created a nation of independent landowners, and the future of the nation certainly pointed to the continued expansion and prosperity of the yeoman class.

At the heart of Jefferson's confidence in the farmer lay his commitment to republicanism. He, more than any other, optimistically believed that the common welfare of the country was intimately connected to and dependent upon the common man. For this reason, Jefferson and others favored laws to protect farmers from land speculators. True wealth resided in productive endeavors, not in land hoarding and speculation. Through hard work on one's own property, a person enriched not only himself but the country as well and helped create a sense of public virtue necessary for the success of the Republic.[1]

This view that the destiny of the country lay in the hands of the small farmers eventually informed American public land policy and the disposal of the public domain. Although policy makers at first believed that monies raised from the sale of the public lands would help support the new government, by about the middle of Andrew Jackson's presidency, many were convinced that the rapid settlement of the federal lands would provide more revenue and at the same time spread the American farmer over a wider area. Land laws, reflecting these ideas, changed to favor settlers' interests. The ultimate expression of the triumph of the settler came in 1862 with the legislative enshrinement of the homestead principle—that is, public land, free of charge, for actual settlement.[2]

The homestead principle had wide public approval in the northern half of the country. By the mid-1850s, the idea of free land for settlement had become a significant element of the new Republican party's ideology, and it bolstered the northern vision of a free capitalist society. That vision was dedicated, in Eric Foner's words, to a belief in "the dignity and opportunities of free labor, and to

1. The history of agrarianism is too well-known to retell here. The best sources are Jefferson himself as well as Gordon Wood, *The Creation of the American Republic, 1776–1787* (Chapel Hill, 1969), 46–124. For an explanation of the theories of agrarianism as American myth, see the classic Henry Nash Smith, *Virgin Land: The American West as Symbol and Myth* (New York, 1950).

2. One of the best summaries of the development of American public land policy remains Benjamin H. Hibbard, *A History of the Public Land Policies* (1924; rpr. Madison, 1965). See also Paul W. Gates, *History of Public Land Law Development* (Washington, D.C., 1969).

social mobility, enterprise, and 'progress.'"[3] To Republicans, the model laborer meant a productive citizen whose goal was self-employment. In a nineteenth-century society so overwhelmingly rural, the yeoman, of course, came in for the greatest praise. Always the foundation of the agrarian myth, the small farmer had become the embodiment of the true American. But in the political context of the 1850s, land signified something more than a symbol for the pure, true American; it was an important means for economic advancement.[4]

Intimately related to this conception of northern free society was the Republican party's view of southern slave society. The South had stood for all those things that the northern vision abhorred—a degraded, poor, subservient labor force, working unproductively (because not for its own advancement) on land owned and controlled extensively by a small, ruling elite. This system violated one of the basic tenets behind Republican free labor ideology, namely, the essential harmony between capital and labor.

During the 1850s, debate over the expansion of slavery into the territories had brought the Republican party into existence. Republicans shaped their antislavery attitudes around their free labor ideology. Slaveowners' competition for free land in the territories threatened the basis of social mobility among the laboring people in the North. Republicans felt that the availability of land fueled America's expansive capitalist society. Once elected to Congress, they helped to give expression to these views by endorsing the homestead principle. Homestead bills became an ideological focus for increasingly severe sectional division before the Civil War.[5]

Until secession, the South's virulent opposition kept Congress from adopting homestead legislation. But not all southerners

3. Eric Foner, *Free Soil, Free Labor, Free Men: The Ideology of the Republican Party Before the Civil War* (New York, 1970); Eric Foner, "Politics, Ideology, and the Origins of the American Civil War," in Eric Foner, *Politics and Ideology in the Age of the Civil War* (New York, 1980), 48. I have relied heavily on his insightful analysis of the components of Republican party ideology.
4. Foner, *Free Soil*, 11–14, 17.
5. *Ibid.*, 54.

united behind the opposition. Five southern states, Alabama, Arkansas, Florida, Louisiana, and Mississippi, contained about 46 million acres of public land, and their congressmen seldom opposed homestead measures. Northern support never made these leaders believe that homesteading threatened their peculiar institution. Rather, they believed that homesteading quite suitably disposed of marginal public land that failed to sell even at the lowest price of twelve and a half cents an acre.[6]

This argument for disposal of the so-called refuse lands undoubtedly explains why southerners from the public land states supported antebellum homestead bills without the fear that they threatened slavery. As a matter of fact, Senator Albert Gallatin Brown of Mississippi frequently combined his support for homesteads with a defense of slavery, insisting that homesteading did not mean the extinction of slavery. The only way to get rid of the poor land, he argued in 1852, was to give it away: "I am for changing the policy so as to give us occupants for our refuse lands. . . . I take this to be true, that without a change of policy we shall never get our poor lands settled. . . . Our lands have all been picked and culled, and the refuse tracts may be peopled under this bill, but never at a cost of $1.25 per acre."[7]

In 1860, the House and Senate passed a homestead measure that President Buchanan vetoed. The southern response was revealing. Only eight senators cast negative votes. All came from slave states, but not one senator from a southern public land state voted against it. In the House, the pattern was different; there, the five public land states divided. Of their twenty votes, three were cast for the bill, six against, but most telling, eleven representatives did not vote. Their

6. Congress passed the Graduation Act in 1854 to dispose of public land that would not sell at the minimum price of $1.25 an acre. The law allowed the price of a tract to decline over a period of years to a minimum of twelve and a half cents an acre in the hope that the land would sell at lower prices. Significantly, only one representative from the southern public land states, from Louisiana, voted against the Graduation Act. *House Journal*, 33rd Cong., 1st Sess., 641–42.

7. *Congressional Globe*, 32nd Cong., 1st Sess., 512 (Appendix).

colleagues from the other slave states were more united: all voted against the bill.[8]

Earnest debate began on a new measure in early 1862 while the nation was embroiled in a bloody civil war. Debate about land matters may seem, at first glance, an inappropriate diversion from the pressing issues of the war, but land disposition continued to remain near the center of national consciousness. Republicans quickly decided that land policy could help to determine the course of the war. Their proposals for confiscation of rebel property followed logically from Republican free labor ideology.

The South's departure from Congress allowed Republicans to impose their will on the country. Their debates made one thing clear: they wanted to use public lands in order to convert the South into an image of the North. Representative William Holman of Indiana singled out the southern public lands: "Would it not be well to infuse, if we may, a little more patriotism into those States?" He expressed his hope that "the stalwart soldiers of your Army will invade, not with the sword, but with the plow and reaping hook, the rich glades of Florida, infusing a new life among a people." This "new life" represented a reaction against southern planters, who were, in the Republicans' free soil outlook, land monopolists. Republicans believed that large planters controlled most of the South's public lands and used them as sources of wealth. John Potter of Wisconsin addressed this view when he added a section to the bill to exclude southern planters from the law's benefits to punish them for perpetrating rebellion.[9]

The final law, which Abraham Lincoln signed on May 20, 1862, opened all federal lands—or at least those under Union control—to actual settlement. It gave a qualified person 160 acres of land free upon payment of a ten-dollar registration fee. The homesteader had

8. The Senate vote on S. 416 (44 to 8) is found in the *Senate Journal*, 36th Cong., 1st Sess., 458. The House vote (118 to 51) is in the *House Journal*, 36th Cong., 1st Sess., 1156–57.

9. *Congressional Globe*, 37th Cong., 2nd Sess., 1031–32, 1035.

to settle and make improvements on the land for five years before he or she could receive title to it. If the settler failed to carry out the requirements, the plot reverted to the government. The last section of the law provided for commutation, that is to say, a person who had homesteaded a quarter section of land could pay the minimum price for it after six months' residency and cultivation, thus bypassing the five-year settlement and cultivation period.[10] But the act represented much more. It reflected the North's thinking about southern landownership. One provision excluded from the law's benefits all persons who had borne arms against the United States. Another required an oath of future loyalty. The law completed the transformation of thinking about the public lands—from a source of revenue to a catalyst for quick settlement. The Homestead Act represented the apotheosis of free soil, free labor Republican ideology.

Because free labor stood at the center of Republican party ideology, the Republican Congress considered various other proposals for land reform during the war, including confiscation, temporary leasing, and even permanent transfer. Before the end of the war, they abandoned confiscation as a solution to the land problem, and within several months after the armistice, President Andrew Johnson's pardoning policies had restored much of the confiscated rebel lands to their former owners.

Except for some minor alterations, congressmen allowed the homestead concept to remain dormant until the end of the war when new and challenging issues confronted the nation. Not the least of these was the future of the almost four million former slaves in southern society. As Leon Litwack has shown, freedom meant many things to them, but one stood above all others: the freedom to carve out independent niches as farmers of their own land. Landownership was the key to black freedom, in the eyes of both blacks and whites, and blacks intensely desired to obtain land. This determination toward independence frightened white southerners, for

10. *Homestead Act, Statutes at Large* (1862), Vol. XII, Chap. 75.

they believed that the plantation economy could not survive with free black labor. So they became just as determined to keep blacks on the plantations. The Black Codes of 1865 expressed best the whites' intentions to preserve the plantation system. Among other things, these laws provided that blacks have jobs for the year, with severe penalties for vagrancy. The Mississippi law even prevented blacks from owning land in rural areas. Taken together, black expectations and white fears underscored the central issue of the post-emancipation South—what Eric Foner has called "labor control and access to economic resources."[11]

After the war, Congress took notice of the remaining federal lands in the southern states. The legislation it passed in February, 1866, to renew the Freedmen's Bureau, which had been set up the year before as a temporary, one-year relief measure, had a provision to dispose of some of the public lands in the southern states. Section Four gave the president the authority to reserve from sale or settlement three million acres of the unoccupied public lands. These were to be allotted in forty-acre tracts to "freedmen and loyal refugees," who were to pay rent on them. After a certain time, the settlers had the option to buy the tracts at a price based on the value of the land. Johnson vetoed this bill; although Congress first sustained his veto, a revised bill became law in July against the president's will. This final measure did not contain the section concerning the public lands, for the Southern Homestead Act, passed a few weeks earlier, preempted that provision.[12]

Both positive and negative considerations shaped the Southern Homestead Act. Many millions of homeless black and white men

11. Leon F. Litwack, *Been in the Storm So Long: The Aftermath of Slavery* (New York, 1979); Eric Foner, *Nothing But Freedom: Emancipation and Its Legacy* (Baton Rouge, 1983), 43.

12. The vetoed Freedmen's Bureau bill can be consulted in Edward McPherson, *A Handbook of Politics for 1868* (Washington, D.C., 1868), 72–74. See also Bentley, *History of the Freedmen's Bureau*, 116; and *Congressional Globe*, 39th Cong., 1st Sess., 209–10. The bill that passed on July 16, 1866, can be consulted in *Freedmen's Bureau Act, Statutes at Large*, Vol. XIV, Chap. 200. LaWanda Cox discusses the formulation and resolution of the provision concerning the public lands in "The Promise of Land for the Freedmen," 413–40.

and women, as Republicans had always insisted, were eager to begin new lives and build new homes in their battered section. The president, whose approval was needed for any legislative action, was a well-known defender of the rights of the small farmer and of the principle of providing homes for the homeless. Above all, by 1866, the homestead principle was a well-woven thread in the nineteenth-century liberal fabric. Free land was not a government handout, but a means by which a person might help himself.

Aside from these positive considerations, the South's enemies believed that the section must be chastised for opposing earlier homestead legislation and causing the war. The planter oligarchy, so the Radicals thought, had withstood attacks upon their land and slaves by blocking legislation that might have established a powerful yeomanry in their midst. Now, Congress could and should dictate to these traitors in no uncertain terms. By peopling the countryside with small farmers, the thinking went, Congress could mold the South into the small-farm image of the rest of America.

What remained of the public domain in the southern states? Would there be enough to fulfill the dreams of the reformers and their beneficiaries? Quantity was only one consideration. The land had to be productive, clearable, and worth the settlers' time and efforts. What was its quality, and where was it located? As might be expected, these questions are difficult to answer with any degree of certainty. Faulty records and an unwieldy system make any definite responses dubious. However, some attempt can be made to derive a well-informed estimate of the quantity, quality, and location of the land. Table 1 compares the amount of unsold public land in the five southern public land states with the total area of the states. Of the 160 million acres of land, over 46 million acres, or 29 percent of the total area, belonged to the federal government. It could dispose of that land as it wanted.

The exact location and topography of these public lands are difficult to determine due to the nature of the public land system. The only official records that indicated land disposition were the town-

TABLE 1
Amount of Public Land in the South

State	Acres of Public Land	Total Area	Percent Public Land
Alabama	6,732,058	32,462,080	20.7
Arkansas	9,298,613	33,406,720	27.8
Florida	19,379,636[a]	37,931,520	51.1
Louisiana	6,228,102[b]	26,461,440	23.5
Mississippi	4,760,736	30,179,840	15.8
	46,399,145	160,441,600	28.9

SOURCE: *Congressional Globe,* 39th Cong., 1st Sess., 715; U.S. Department of Interior, General Land Office, *Report of the Commissioner of the General Land Office,* 1866, p. 57.
[a]11,300,000 acres were as yet unsurveyed.
[b]3,000,000 acres were as yet unsurveyed.

ship plats.[13] Generally, the federal domain was any land that had not passed into private hands or that had not been donated to the states for various reasons. These different sections formed a patchwork quilt on the map of the state.

Most of the quality land in the five public land states had already been claimed and settled before the war. The remaining public domain was largely the refuse lands, worthless for any suitable settlement and cultivation, because the tracts remained unsold even when their price had reached the minimum level of twelve and a half cents an acre. In 1860, the five southern public land states had a total of 50,510,000 acres available for sale as refuse land. In fact, Arkansas and Alabama led the rest of the country in total acres of refuse land.[14] Since there were 46 million acres of public land in

13. There are no state maps that reliably indicate public land locations because the extent and locations change so frequently. The township plats may be found in Cartographic Records, Legislative and Natural Resources Branch, Record Group 49, National Archives, Washington, D.C.
14. *House Executive Documents,* 34th Cong., 1st Sess., No. 13, p. 570.

1866, one could assume that most of it was of poor quality for farming.

On January 8, 1866, John H. Rice of Maine introduced legislation to dispose of the public lands in the South. The bill was short. Simply stated, it proposed extending the 1862 Homestead Act to the South with two exceptions: a person could enter only eighty acres, and homesteading was the only way that the public lands could be given away in the southern states.[15]

No one man fought harder for the dispersal of land to the freedmen than George W. Julian, Indiana congressman and chairman of the House Committee on Public Lands. Julian had his ideological grounding as an abolitionist and Free-Soiler and was one of the leading Radical Republicans. Later, he became identified with the Liberal wing of the Republican party and ended his career as a Cleveland Democrat. A true friend of reform and a supporter of various social reform groups, Julian adeptly incorporated land matters into his social and political ideology. Believing that the southern landed aristocracy in particular and land monopolists and speculators in general obstructed the goals of free labor, Julian decided that using the public lands to halt these menaces was one way of achieving his radical ends. To put it another way, Julian desired to place only settlers on the public lands in order to brake capitalist and corporate grabbing.[16]

Convinced that southern planters were not only the largest land hoarders in the country but traitors as well, he desired to see their

15. H.R. 85, *A Bill for the Disposal of the Public Lands for Homestead Actual Settlement in the States of Alabama, Mississippi, Louisiana, Arkansas and Florida*, January 8, 1866, 39th Cong., 1st Sess. Summary of action on H.R. 85, 39th Cong., 1st Sess.: *House Journal*, 113, 245, 845, 899; *Senate Journal*, 147, 335, 347, 379, 457.

16. Patrick W. Riddleberger, "George W. Julian: Abolitionist Land Reformer," *Agricultural History*, XXIX (1955), 108–10. Julian corresponded with several women in the feminist movement, including Elizabeth Cady Stanton, Lucy Stone, and Julia Ward Howe, all of whom had sought his support. He also had introduced a bill in 1865 that would have extended the suffrage to the black people of Washington, D.C. See the Joshua Giddings (George W. Julian) Papers, III–IV, Library of Congress. See also *Congressional Globe*, 39th Cong., 1st Sess., 19; Paul W. Gates, "Federal Land Policy in the South, 1866–1888," *Journal of Southern History*, VI (1940), 304–306.

lands confiscated and distributed to Union soldiers as homesteads. This was truly radical thinking, for it involved, first, the seizure of private land, second, the transfer of land to black Americans, and third, a suspicion of corporations. All were new variants of the Jeffersonian vision.

Frustrated during the war in his attempts to distribute rebel lands to loyal persons, Julian prepared for the next round shortly after the opening of the Thirty-ninth Congress.[17] He sent a letter to the commissioner of the General Land Office, James Edmunds, asking his views on certain questions. Edmunds responded on February 5, 1866, with ammunition for Julian's bill, which was already pending in the House. After informing the congressman of the amount of public land, Edmunds assembled figures that indicated that a very small elite in the South controlled most of the section's lands. By combining population figures with agricultural holdings, the commissioner concluded that large unproductive landowners monopolized over 50 million acres of land. In brief, the five southern public land states in 1860 had about 160,000 farms covering an area of almost 57 million acres. Only about 17 million of those acres, or 30 percent, were improved. The remaining 104 million acres were not in farms and were unimproved. The surveyed and unsurveyed federal lands accounted for half that figure. The remainder, Edmunds concluded, formed "part of the land monopoly in those States." This land, he said, was controlled by states and corporations who had been given grants "and by individuals not engaged in agricultural pursuits."

The commissioner went on to combine the population and farm data, estimating the total number of landowners outside of towns to be about 200,000. If we assume that each represented a five-member family, 1 million people had a direct interest in the land. That left 2 million, more than two-thirds of the population, landless. Edmunds

17. For the war, see *Congressional Globe,* 38th Cong., 1st Sess., 874. For a fuller discussion of Julian's legislation, see Roy M. Robbins, *Our Landed Heritage: The Public Domain, 1776–1936* (Princeton, 1942), 210–11.

underscored his point by noting that the South's primary occupation was agriculture, yet only one-tenth of the land was improved.[18]

The debates in the winter and spring addressed the twin issues of assisting the freedmen and punishing the rebels. Julian took the floor on February 7. Finally abandoning his hopes of confiscating rebel lands, he admitted that the proposed bill would not have been necessary, had an extensive confiscation plan passed. A southern homestead law was needed now more than ever because black people needed homes. Making more land available would create, in true Republican phraseology, "a wider field for free labor." In order to provide that "wider field," homesteads could be only 80 acres instead of 160. Julian explained that the reduced acreage was essential because of "the increased necessity for homesteads in that section of [the] country caused by the abolition of slavery and the demands of free labor." Over 46 million acres of public land would provide about 586,000 homesteads. If each homestead supported an average of 5 persons, the needs of 2,931,000 southerners could be served. Representative Rice pointed out that, even if only 30 million acres were suitable for cultivation, 1,875,000 people would be supported. He interjected that land belonging to Confederate states but not reverting to the federal government through conquest should have been confiscated. This would have added, for example, 100 million acres of public land in Texas that had never been a part of the public domain. The bill's sponsors were obviously aware that not everyone who wanted land in the South would be able to get it under this legislation. In regard to numbers, they were not such starry-eyed reformers.[19]

Julian used the commissioner's views about southern land monopoly to support his personal view that landowners must live on their property in order to halt land speculation. "Rebel spec-

18. Land Commissioner James Edmunds to George W. Julian, February 5, 1866, in *Congressional Globe,* 39th Cong., 1st Sess., 715. There were 46 million acres of surveyed public land and 5 million of unsurveyed land. The sum total accounts for about half of the remaining 104 million acres that were not in farms and unimproved.

19. *Congressional Globe,* 39th Cong., 1st Sess., 715–17.

ulators," he said, were "hovering" over the section, waiting to take the best of the land "at one swoop and cheat the actual settler, whether black or white, out of his rights, or even the possibility of a home to come in that region."[20]

In making the case that free land was a strong weapon against speculation, Julian linked the arguments for the southern homestead bill with the commonly accepted view that landownership was the basis of economic strength and freedom. John Rice, the bill's sponsor, stated the point even more forcefully. The southern states, he said, were characterized by land monopolies supported by the slaveowning element, and it was now time to establish "liberty, right, and justice" in the South. He was convinced that the protection of the poor from "the wrongs and oppressions of capital and aristocracy" was the most important and most difficult problem of the century, and he saw its solution in both political and social terms. The pending legislation would rip the public domain "forever from the rapacious talons of the monopolist and the speculators" and distribute it to those who deserved it—"the oppressed, wronged, and suffering poor." By owning their own land, laboring people could support themselves economically and have the means to defend themselves against encroachments by employers. "No man can be made a slave so long as he has the means to support himself," Rice affirmed.[21]

John Rice put his arguments squarely in the middle of the traditional thinking. The homestead principle evoked dreams of utopia—where small farmers held their own land, worked hard, maintained a strong, independent economic position, and lived out the American dream. In short, a homestead was a panacea, able to solve all pressing problems or at least strengthen the moral fiber of the homesteader so he could deal with them.

But the thinking ignored something fundamental for any possible success of this free soil scheme. Rice never gave much thought to the location or quality of the land; he considered only ownership impor-

20. *Ibid.*, 716.
21 *Ibid.*, 716–17.

tant. "Where ever and whenever [the laboring classes] can have homes and lands of their own," he pointed out, "even if they be in the mountains and amid the swamps, there human nature and human manhood will assert its prerogatives and its freedom."[22] This argument contained nothing new; it implied that the disadvantaged would be able to procure justice on their own simply by possessing land.

What was new about the Southern Homestead Act were its primary beneficiaries, the landless freedmen. Previous homestead legislation either implied Negro exclusion or specifically excluded black people. When Roger Taney ruled in the Dred Scott decision that Negroes were not citizens, he effectively excluded blacks from the benefits of any future homestead law, because all of them restricted homesteading to citizens. True, some whites could homestead under the Southern Homestead Act, but not all could, because the 1862 law had excluded any rebels from its benefits.[23]

If Confederates were excluded, then the majority of homesteaders in the southern states would be black. Put differently, the measure was a way of providing Negroes with a necessary economic foundation while at the same time punishing rebels. Julian appreciated the full impact it might have and made a strong effort to secure black people in their rights to the land. While the bill was in committee, he added a provision which stated that "no distinction or discrimination shall be made in the construction or execution of this act on account of race or color." This clause remained a part of the bill and is significant because it was the first time that any legislation included such a stipulation. Julian explained his reason for including it by taking a stab at the Democratic party: "In consequence of the Dred Scott decision, and the power of latter-day Democracy in debauching the public sentiment of the country, it is not generally understood that black men have any rights in relation to the public domain of the country. . . . I believe it is now unknown to

22. *Ibid.*, 716.
23. *Homestead Act, Statutes at Large* (1862), Vol. XII, Chap. 75, Sec. 1.

multitudes of white men, even in the northern States, that colored men have any rights under the homestead law [1862]. We ought to make that fact known to black and white, so that the multitudes of landless people may understand what are their rights of acquiring homesteads."[24]

The southern homestead bill passed the House of Representatives on February 8 by a roll-call vote of 112 to 29. Forty-one men did not vote. Significantly, all Democrats voted against the bill, and all but three Republicans voted for it. New York, New Jersey, Pennsylvania, and Kentucky had less than 50 percent of their votes recorded as yea, nay, or not voting. Sixty percent of Maryland's representatives did not vote. Delaware's only representative voted in the negative. It should also be observed that thirteen Democrats and twenty-eight Republicans did not vote. That is, 33 percent of the Democrats and 20 percent of the Republicans chose not to be counted, for one reason or another. Despite this overall lower Republican percentage, a higher percentage of Republicans did not vote in Maryland, one of the border states. Also, in New York, approximately the same percentages of Republicans and Democrats did not vote (38 percent and 40 percent). More than this, of the twenty-five states in the Union, fourteen, or 56 percent, had no Democratic representatives. So although the vote was partisan, other factors tend to soften this particular interpretation.[25]

The Senate proposed several amendments to H.R. 85 that had the effect of lessening its impact on southern whites. One excluded timberlands from homesteading.[26] Mineral lands had already been excluded. This particular amendment was killed before the bill's final passage; had it remained, the amount of public land available for homesteading would have been substantially reduced in some states. On the other hand, the restriction might have helped to keep lumbermen honest, for with no distinction drawn in classification

24. H.R. 85, February 7, 1866; *Congressional Globe,* 39th Cong., 1st Sess., 716.
25. *Congressional Globe,* 39th Cong., 1st Sess., 718.
26. *Ibid.,* 2735. See also H.R. 85 (April 13, 1866), lines 20–21.

between timberlands and cultivable lands, lumbering interests filed false homestead claims for the sole purpose of stripping the land of its valuable timber.

A second proposed amendment had greater ramifications, at least as far as southerners were concerned. Added to the bill was a section that radically changed the 1862 law for the South. The earlier legislation specifically excluded Confederates, but the bill pending in 1866 would open the southern public lands to all people, Union or Confederate, black or white. Senator Samuel Pomeroy, chairman of the Senate Public Lands Committee, explained that the purpose of this section was to allow "poor men who had been engaged in the rebellion" to get eighty acres by pledging future allegiance to the Union. Rebel elements who were not plantation owners would have the opportunity to avail themselves of the public lands. This attempt at moderation would also attract more support for the bill.[27]

The Senate agreed to another amendment that made the Homestead Act of 1862 and its subsequent amendments applicable to the 1866 bill "as fully as if herein enacted and set forth."[28] The effect was to make the proposed law a supplement to the 1862 Homestead Act.

Much of the debate in the Senate concerned the provision that restricted homesteads to 80 acres. Thomas Hendricks, Democrat from Indiana, expressed the most opposition to the 80-acre restriction, believing that a uniform policy of 160 acres was fairer. Samuel Kirkwood of Iowa, voicing another objection to the 80-acre limitation, said that immigrants would not be attracted to the South because they could get more land in the West. "Although I may not agree with some Senators in regard to some matters concerning these seceded States," he stated, "I certainly do not desire to do them any injustice; I do not desire to take any action that will injure their material interests."[29]

27. *Congressional Globe,* 39th Cong., 1st Sess., 2735.
28. *Ibid.* See also H.R. 85 (April 27, 1866), Sec. 3.
29. *Congressional Globe,* 39th Cong., 1st Sess., 2735. On the need for immigrants, see Foner, *Nothing But Freedom,* 47–49.

In replying to his colleague's objections, Pomeroy pointedly clarified the bill's purpose. The South, he said, contained a large population of loyal Negroes who heretofore had been barred from the public lands. Also, white people held most of the best southern lands in large estates. Then, in no uncertain terms, he stated, "The object of this bill is to cut the public land up into small homesteads; and it need not be disguised that it is aimed particularly for the benefit of the colored man, those who have not been able hitherto to acquire homesteads on the public domain in these States." Pomeroy knew that the recently freed slaves "must have a footing in the soil." He also believed that former masters would not sell lands to their former slaves. Even if the masters were magnanimous, the freedmen did not have the means to buy the land. "They have been stripped of everything. True, thank God! they are free, but they have nothing but their hands to rely upon for support, and they want land." Pomeroy even went so far as to say that the federal government had an obligation to see that Negroes got land before immigrants, because Negroes had been loyal but never had been allowed to become landowners. The senator pointed out that the southern lands had been on the market for a long time, and yet few, if any, foreigners had been attracted to them. He firmly declared that "the object of this bill is to let [Negroes] have the land in preference to people from Europe or anybody else."[30]

A House-Senate conference committee met to work out the differences between the two houses. The Chicago *Tribune* reported on June 4 that the three senators on the committee supported the Senate amendment, requiring the oath of future, but not past, allegiance, but that Julian and Rice felt "that the privilege of setting upon the public domain should not be given to rebels." The committee resolved their differences by mid-June, and both houses approved the report.[31]

30. *Congressional Globe*, 39th Cong., 1st Sess., 2735–36.

31. The members of the committee for the Senate were Samuel J. Kirkwood (Republican of Iowa), Henry Wilson (Republican of Massachusetts), and Garret Davis (Democrat of Kentucky). The final members for the House were George W. Julian

The southern homestead bill went to the president as a painfully compromised measure. The houses adjusted their disagreements by setting time limits on the restrictions. The final bill let stand the 80-acre restriction, but only for two years; after mid-1868, settlers could get 160-acre homesteads. The Senate gave up the inclusion of its timberlands provision, thereby excluding only mineral lands from the law. This particular omission was to have far-reaching effects on the southern forests.

Perhaps the most important condition was also compromised. The House gave in on the question of rebel landownership. The final measure retained intact the Senate's section, opening the lands to former Confederates. However, a provision added at the end of the section directed that all those who applied for land by January 1, 1867, had to swear that they had not borne arms against the United States or given aid and comfort to its enemies.[32]

Was this particular clause designed to give freedmen a head start? Senator Kirkwood explained that the committee had agreed on a January 1 date because "much the larger portion" of the freedmen had contracted their labor for the year. Because they must honor their contracts, the freedmen would not be able to take advantage of the Southern Homestead Act until January 1, when their contracts expired. The restrictions on former Confederates should be retained "until the time when the freedmen will be in a position to avail themselves of the benefit of this law."[33] In short, the purpose of the provision was to allow black and white southerners access to the

---

(Republican of Indiana), John Rice (Republican of Maine), and Syndenham E. Ancona (Democrat of Pennsylvania). *Congressional Globe*, 39th Cong., 1st Sess., 2771, 2852; *Biographical Directory of the American Congress* (Washington, D.C., 1971); Chicago *Tribune*, June 4, 1866.

32. *Congressional Globe*, 30th Cong., 1st Sess., 3166.

33. *Ibid.*, 3179. Christine Farnham Pope, in "Southern Homesteads for Negroes," *Agricultural History*, XLIV (1970), 201–12, admits that the Senate put in the six-month period to help blacks fulfill their contracts. But Warren Hoffnagle, in "The Southern Homestead Act: Its Origins and Operation," *Historian*, XXXII (1970), 616, does not say why Congress shaped that section as it did. He assumes it was to allay fears that the law without the restriction discriminated in favor of Negroes.

land at the same time; it was not intended to give black people a six-month advantage.

Reaction to the Southern Homestead Act was scant, considering the major implications and policy change that it signaled. Some newspapers, like the Huntsville, Alabama, *Advocate,* merely reported that the bill had been signed. Others, like the New Orleans *Times,* published the act in full without comment. The Vicksburg *Daily Herald* announced the details of the bill after it had passed the House in February under the telling headline, "The Freedmen's Homestead Law." In July, the same paper published a circular pertaining to the act under headlines that made the editor's sentiments clear: "Colonizing Negroes in Mississippi."[34]

Most newspapers, whether their editorial opinions toward the act were favorable or unfavorable, believed that the act would make former slaves landowners. Both the New York *Tribune* and the New York *World* called it the "Negro Homestead Bill." The Memphis *Daily Commercial,* quoting the St. Louis *Republican,* said the act was "intended entirely for the benefit of the negroes."[35]

Most of the approbation came from northern papers. They saw the act as the Republican framers did: the means by which the southern people could contribute to the welfare of their own region by converting the South into a section of small farms cultivated by owners, both black and white. The New York *Tribune* editorialized in early February that the pending legislation might "prevent pauperism, . . . counteract unfriendly legislation in reference to the negro, and . . . open a pathway for industry and honest trial." After the final bill passed in mid-June, the editor held it to be "one of the best practical measures of reconstruction yet enacted."[36]

The most extensive and insightful comments from a northern paper came from the radical Boston *Daily Advertiser.* In an article

34. Huntsville *Advocate,* June 30, 1866; New Orleans *Times,* July 8, 1866; Vicksburg *Daily Herald,* February 15, July 7, 1866.

35. New York *Tribune,* February 9, 1866; New York *World,* June 16, 1866; Memphis *Daily Commercial,* quoting the St. Louis *Republican,* July 8, 1866.

36. New York *Tribune,* February 9, June 15, 1866.

entitled "Practical Reconstruction," the writer referred to the Southern Homestead Act as the most important measure passed during the last session of Congress. He felt that the Freedmen's Bureau had "no better opportunity for inestimable usefulness since its establishment." The law would solve the social and political problems of the South in a practical way. He explained, "It will break down the land monopoly of the ex-slaveholding classes of the South, that has been the root of slavery and rebellion. It will, by enabling the poor whites and emancipated slaves to become possessors of lands in their own rights and to pursue the road to independence and wealth, work a complete regeneration in the South of a few years. It will redeem the immense wastes of that favored land and, by developing its untouched resources, add vastly to the national affluence and prosperity."[37]

In its editorial, the *Daily Advertiser* provided a somewhat extended analysis of the effects of the legislation and perceived more realistically than others the indirect consequences. The writer first congratulated the president for signing the measure, for his action proved, more than anything else, Johnson's willingness to help the freedmen, a sentiment he had expressed when he vetoed the Freedmen's Bureau bill. His signature was also consistent with his support of early homestead measures. But still, the writer speculated, Johnson might have vetoed the bill, claiming it was special legislation, something he had also asserted in his veto of the second Freedmen's Bureau bill.

The writer then utilized Republican free soil, free labor ideology. The legislation would help create a southern yeomanry, he believed, although he was not convinced that landownership was the best means to accomplish this end: "It must be admitted that the end [a yeoman class] would be better reached if it were possible for each man to earn his farm for himself, as our New England farmers do." He went so far as to say that most of the former slaves would be better off working for wages rather than cultivating their own lands

37. Boston *Daily Advertiser,* June 23, 1866. The Chicago *Tribune* of June 21, 1866, printed the same correspondence, which was dated June 16, 1866.

because they needed "the discipline of a steady and gradual rise from their degraded position."[38]

As far as utopia developing in the South, the paper was more realistic than optimistic. The writer believed that the act would have no effect in breaking up the southern aristocracy, because the yeomanry would be isolated on the public lands, undoubtedly far from the "real seats of aristocracy." But he expressed optimism: the effect of the bill would be "in establishing a democratic community *by the side* of the aristocratic." Although he did not believe this situation ideal, the writer thought it a step in the right direction, for labor, unleashed from its subservience to capital and without the "outward intervention of a bureau or court, which might be regarded as temporary and abnormal," could eventually become "absolute and conscious master of its own situation." With labor scarce and small farms available, the former slave and the former master could enter into "a desirable relationship." Also, the right to a homestead would provide security for the freedmen against mistreatment and fraud. Landowners would begin to appreciate the benefits of selling small plots of land at low rates to their laborers in order to keep them in the area. The writer concluded, "We shall thus have a genuine and well-organized yeomanry, formed by a healthy growth, not by any forcing process; scattered in among the large estates, and not set apart by themselves."[39]

This last argument proceeded from the old notion that land meant security and freedom and was thus a defense against fraud and oppression. The Chicago *Tribune* adopted this same premise, but stated it negatively. The editor pointed out that the opponents of the act, "the enemies of freedom," were frightened that their slaves would become landholders and self-supporting, thus removing a much-needed labor supply. The writer explained, "This proceeds upon the old slaveholders' supposition that the cotton crop is of more importance than the men who raise it." He then attempted to refute an opposing argument: "Experience shows that most labor

38. Boston *Daily Advertiser,* July 10, 1866.
39. *Ibid.*

is performed in those communities where landholders are most numerous, and all have a motive to work."[40]

Democratic papers, North and South, had their doubts. They reiterated the often-heard tenet that Negroes were lazy and would not work unless they were supervised. The New York *World,* for example, described the Southern Homestead Act as "a bill to get rid of the laboring class." The Memphis *Appeal* adopted a similar stance. In an article reproduced in the Vicksburg *Daily Herald* on July 17, 1866, the writer called the act "one of the most sinister blows aimed at the industry of the Southern people." He explicated: "Those who begot and brought this new law into the world, we may rest assured, design by attentive nursing to make it a syren which shall destroy Southern industry by seducing the negro away from his old fields of labor—the cotton fields. . . . Should our negroes be inveigled away, and led to set up these homestead farms to any great extent, they will thereafter produce little cotton or sugar; but simply corn, and vegetables, and meat enough for their own uses, and nothing more, to the sad prejudice, if not utter ruin of cotton culture." To counter this effect, the author urged planters to improve relations in order to satisfy the Negroes on their plantations.[41]

The Memphis *Daily Commercial* went beyond the *Appeal* and declared that most of the black homesteaders would become "slovenly squatters." It maintained that, as a class, Negroes were "indolent, and lacking in foresight, fond of amusing themselves, and devoting to the pleasures of a gossipping intercourse time which ought to be spent in productive industry." Because of these unique traits, the reformers' actions were "about equal to that of extracting sunbeams from cucumbers."[42]

One southern paper, the Little Rock *Daily Gazette,* expressed a different concern. Knowing all too well the desire of the former

40. Chicago *Tribune,* June 30, 1866.

41. New York *World,* June 26, 1866; Memphis *Appeal* in Vicksburg *Daily Herald,* July 17, 1866.

42. Memphis *Daily Commercial,* July 8, 1866.

slaves to have land, the paper feared that the large amounts of land in Arkansas would attract too many Negroes. With the availability and low cost that the act provided, black people "will swarm . . . from the other States." The writer also feared that the six-month exclusive period would cause some black people to break their contracts "and thus seriously injure, if not destroy farming interests for the present year."[43]

Significantly, only the southern press gave warning about the quality of the public lands the Southern Homestead Act would open for homesteading. While the measure was still under debate, the Mobile *Daily Advertiser and Register* pointed out, rather facetiously, that the most humane feature of the bill was its eighty-acre restriction. The writer said there were not eighty acres in Alabama on which a settler "would not starve and be taxed to death in three weeks. Make it the Homestead allowance of 160 acres, and imagine the poor devil's fate!" The Jackson *Daily Mississippi Clarion and Standard,* more circumspect and prophetic, surmised that only about one-tenth of the available acreage was fit for cultivation. Most of the public land, the editor said, was piney woods, good for hunting and fishing, "but on which a laboring man would starve."[44]

The press views underscored the thinking of both sides. Proponents saw the Southern Homestead Act as one means to remake the South into the image of the North. Opponents saw the end of cotton cultivation as they knew it, because the promise of free land would lure away the work force. The measure did not embrace the most radical of Republican proposals, the confiscation or redistribution of land, but its intentions were still a bold departure in American history. It tried to extend the resources of public land to black Americans and draw them into the American mainstream. It is true that the act's architects presumed that a southern farmer class did not exist; and it is also true that southerners really believed that the

43. Little Rock *Daily Gazette,* July 11, 1866.
44. Mobile *Daily Advertiser and Register,* February 12, 1866; Jackson *Daily Mississippi Clarion and Standard,* July 7, 1866.

law would mean their economic ruin. Laws passed, of course, do not necessarily mean dreams or nightmares realized. The application and enforcement of the Southern Homestead Act would tell the real story.

II

Getting Down to Business

Reconstruction issues were diverse and complex, but political ones stood front and center of most questions. To understand the land issue and, more particularly, the operation of the Southern Homestead Act, one must understand the politics that shaped it and ultimately determined its history. Put differently, one of the most crucial political questions of the era was who would control the economic resources and means of production in the Reconstruction South. The drafters of the Southern Homestead Act tried to answer that question, but the extent that the legislation delivered on its drafters' promises depended, in large measure, on those whose job it was to enforce the law. The president's appointments provided the political context for the distribution of the federal lands; the General Land Office interpreted the law; the land officers administered the law locally. All determined whether or not the land office machinery was well greased.

The Interior Department oversaw the federal lands through its agency, the General Land Office, which was headed by a commissioner. Below the commissioner were two officials in each local land district—a register who recorded land entries and a receiver who collected monies. The Interior Department carried with it a long list of patronage offices, including the General Land Office. In the South, every position had to be filled after the war. Specifically, the reopening and reorganization of the offices in the southern public land states first required the appointments of registers and receivers, both of whom had to be in service to transact business. In some states, if federal lands remained unsurveyed, it was necessary to appoint a surveyor general. Eventually each office was opened, but for the ten years that the Southern Homestead Act was on the books, not all offices were operating efficiently and effectively.

The generally mediocre caliber of the officers accounted, in large part, for the lax execution of the law. Andrew Johnson's appointments followed the time-honored tradition of Jacksonian politics. Theoretically in charge of the vast federal patronage, the president of the United States, by 1865, was limited by important practical political considerations, not the least of which were the advisory channels of the federal and state representatives, governors, political bosses, and department heads.[1] Most of the applicants for the two land office posts stressed their party loyalties and their devotion to their federal representatives, the key figures in making recommendations and nominations. Very few listed any previous experience with land questions. Depending on the presidential administration or the state government in power, sectional affiliation might prove influential; some senators, for example, did not want to nominate nonsoutherners. Factional Republican infighting also provided a colorful context for the conducting of official business, and more often than not, the local land office position was merely the first step on the ladder to a career in state politics.

The most important criterion for holding office was loyalty to the administration in power. In 1866, J. A. Shrigley was well qualified to be receiver in Clarksville, Arkansas, because he "endors[es] the great principles of Reconstruction advocated by that great man Andrew Johnson." He got the job, thus indicating that presidential Reconstruction, Johnson style, would hold sway in Clarksville during Shrigley's tenure. Senator B. F. Rice underlined the primary importance of loyalty to the current administration when the term of John Kirkwood, a Johnson appointee, expired in 1870. In strongly

1. James L. Baumgardner, "Andrew Johnson and the Patronage" (Ph.D. dissertation, University of Tennessee, 1968), 10–11.

recommending Rollins Edgerton as receiver in Little Rock, Rice explained to the GLO, "There is no good reason for the removal of John Kirkwood except the single fact that he is a democrat and furiously opposed reconstruction, while Mr. Edgerton whom we recommend is a steadfast republican, and an elegant business man."[2] The recommendation indicated not only the change in administration but also the direction in which the regular wing of the Republican party was moving.

Johnson's consideration of officers in Florida rested upon the Conservative-Radical feud, with all candidates vying for the Conservative label. Charles Mundee, a relatively new resident of Tallahassee, was competing with Henry DeAhna, former special agent for the GLO. Several citizens of Tallahassee, with the endorsement of Governor David Walker, informed Johnson that Mundee's appointment would be "favorable to the early settlement of our difficulties." The editor of the Tallahassee *Semi-Weekly Floridian,* C. E. Dyke, a Democrat, also supported Mundee's appointment. Dyke, who knew Mundee "would not use [his] influence against the whites," asked Johnson to take under advisement the seriousness of local appointments, especially in order to maintain presidential policies on the local level.

The other candidate, DeAhna, also played on the political issue, stating that he was "*no Radical,*" but that Mundee had become one. DeAhna, who described Tallahassee as "a sickly hole with chills and fever raging all the time," did not get the job. Johnson named Mundee, who, unlike Kirkwood in Arkansas, proved suitable enough to survive the change in administrations, for Florida's representatives urged Grant to retain him. He remained in office until 1871, but then resigned because of charges that he was working against congressional Reconstruction. His critics charged that his

2. John S. Houston to John M. Oliver, October 3, 1866, B. F. Rice to W. F. Otto, February 3, 1870, both in Appointments Division, Appointment Papers, U.S. Land Officers, Arkansas, Office of the Secretary of the Interior, Record Group 48, National Archives.

appointment had come upon the recommendation of William Marvin, "late rebel senator elect," and David Walker, "late rebel governor of Florida."[3]

The Reconstruction career of the surveyor general of Florida best illustrates the divisive nature of state politics and the vicissitudes of political affiliations. Marcellus L. Stearns became the first surveyor general after the war when Grant named him in April, 1869. His appointment was only the first step in a career that would bring him to the governor's chair, and it would not take long. By early 1870, Republican governor Harrison Reed had some doubt about Stearns's support of his administration. Reed believed Stearns was "in collusion with certain disaffected republicans and democrats in the Legislature to suspend the Governor, and place one of their number—'ring'—in the Gubernatorial chair—and thereby jeopardize, if not entirely subvert, republican government in Florida." Undoubtedly due to political pressure, Stearns eventually resigned from office, but within four years he became governor of Florida (1874–1877)—the last Republican to serve before the Democrats resumed power.[4]

If history sometimes comes full circle, then events in Florida fit the pattern. In the second year of Stearns's term, former governor Reed expressed concern over the course that Republican politics had taken. He accused his immediate successor, Ossian B. Hart, of having lost the Republican majority and feared that if something were not done, Florida would soon go completely Democratic. How

3. Petition of citizens to Andrew Johnson, August 28, 1867, C. E. Dyke to Andrew Johnson, October 19, 1867, Henry C. DeAhna to Joseph Wilson, September 10, 1867, DeAhna to Jacob Cox, September 6, 1867, T. W. Osborn, A. Gilbert, and Charles Hamilton to Grant, March 19, 1869, all in Appointments, Florida. There are similar charges of Democratic sympathies in a letter from the secretary of the Republican State Executive Committee to Osborn and Gilbert on January 16, 1871, in Appointments, Florida.

4. C. M. Hamilton to Interior Secretary Cox, January 24, 1870, in Appointments, Florida. Joe M. Richardson, *The Negro in the Reconstruction of Florida, 1865–1877* (Tallahassee, 1965), 200. Richardson points out that Stearns was not very "Radical"; he appointed many native whites and few Negroes.

did Reed hope to regain Republican ascendancy? "A prompt and judicious use of the federal patronage & the appointment of only true republicans of character & influence, will stay the tide & save the state to the Republican party." And which position did he have in mind? The surveyor general's office "may be made a power for good in sustaining the waning strength of the republican principles & the republican party." And who did he believe could best fill that position? Himself, of course. And why? "I have presented the only instance of reconstruction of a southern state without resort to martial law or even military assistances, the only state where the free school system has been inaugurated & sustained without violence & a civil rights bill has been enacted & fully acquiesced in throughout; the only state too where a mountain of debt has not been rolled up as a monument of injustice & oppression."[5] Reed never got the job, but his complaints illustrate the nature of political appointments: loyalty to the administration was held in the highest regard. The cases of Stearns and Reed also demonstrate the interrelatedness of state and federal politics.

Politics in Louisiana during Reconstruction has been described as "stormy days" by one of the participants. The term might have been used for all the former Confederate states, because there are similarities in most of them. If Louisiana was different from the others, it was in the persistence and exaggeration of problems that occurred elsewhere. For example, the South's particular habit of placing former Confederates in office persisted through the Grant administration and extended to patronage positions in the land office. Grant named J. Jules Bossier receiver in the Natchitoches land office in mid-1870. When the commissioner wondered why Bossier did not execute his bond, Bossier replied that he could not do so until he was pardoned. By April, 1871, he had subscribed to the oath, executed his bond, and been commissioned. In just over a year, several Louisiana officials requested his removal for a number of

5. Harrison Reed to Columbus Delano, February 16, 1875, in Appointments, Florida.

reasons, among them, a charge that "he is an earnest advocate of the Warmoth party"—and thus opposed to William P. Kellogg, head of the Grant Republicans in Louisiana.[6]

Republican infighting also characterized Mississippi politics in the mid-1870s. The friction arose because the Republican register in Jackson, Richard Kerr, was a native southerner. In February, 1874, Governor Adelbert Ames, Lieutenant Governor A. K. Davis, and black Superintendent of Education T. W. Cardozo urged Grant to replace Kerr with Eugene McMichael, "a deserving, hard working Republican, in harmony with both the present National and State Administrations." The counterclaims attesting to Kerr's staunch Republicanism began pouring into Washington. Congressman George McKee, a northerner who was beginning to desert the Ames ship, stood up for Kerr, defending him against a governor who wanted Kerr removed simply because he did not like him. As McKee put it, "Too much centralization and *State Ceasarism* in that idea."[7]

In checking Kerr's record, the GLO commissioner found his Jackson agent "a faithful and efficient officer," and Lieutenant Governor Davis, recanting his earlier recommendation, now lent his full support to Kerr's retention. Davis' reversal reflected deeper disagreements between Ames and his lieutenant governor, but the support Kerr received from the previous Mississippi governor, James L. Alcorn, was an even more compelling example of the continual feuding between Alcorn and Ames. Alcorn was convinced that the only reason the governor wanted Kerr removed was that the receiver was a southerner. Kerr was certainly the favorite of the state Republican organization, with support from twenty-six senators and sixty-six

6. GLO to J. Jules Bossier, December 17, 1870, in Letters Sent. Bossier responded on December 18, 1870. GLO Commissioner Drummond to Secretary Delano, March 3, 1871, Drummond to Delano, March 3, 1871, both in Division "C," Letters Sent to Other Government Departments, RG 49; GLO to Bossier, April 5, 1871, in Letters Sent; several Louisiana officials to Grant, May 13, 1872, in Appointments, Louisiana.

7. Recommendation in behalf of Eugene McMichael to U. S. Grant, February 10, 1874, signed by A. Ames, A. K. Davis, and T. W. Cardozo, in Appointments, Mississippi, microfilm edition, M849, Reel 3, RG 48; Resolution of Republicans of Jackson, February 14, 1874, George C. McKee to C. Delano, February 16, 1874, both in M849, Reel 2.

representatives. Alcorn did not want the southern Republicans slapped in the face with Kerr's removal, and he took one more jab at Ames when he told the secretary of the interior: "The effort to displace him is in the interest of one who has no identity with the people of our State." The Alcorn faction won this one; Kerr retained his post. In 1877, Senator Blanche K. Bruce urged his reappointment. Indeed, he remained register until he died in 1891.[8]

If northern Republicans were trying to remove southern Republicans in 1874, the tables had turned by 1877. With the Hayes ascendancy came the beginnings of an attempt to maintain a southern Republican party. That would become more difficult as the South became solidly Democratic, but black and white Republicans could still get elected by fusion with independents or displaced Democrats. One way to build the southern Republican party in the South was to trust it to the hands of southern Republicans. Events at the land office in Mobile demonstrated the tactic. C. F. Stearns had occupied the register's office since Grant appointed him in April, 1869. When his second term was almost over in early 1877, his removal was recommended. Why? "He unfortunately belongs to that class of men known as Carpet baggers—whose presence in the South is a perpetual source of irritation. No good man wishes these people any harm—but republicanism can never get on its feet again in the South, till the Carpet baggers give way to active Southern men."[9] Southern governments in southern hands had become the new cry, and the federal government willingly acquiesced.

Political factionalism in Arkansas had immediate consequences for the land office in Little Rock when rivalry between Elisha Baxter and Joseph Brooks erupted into the Brooks-Baxter War in the spring of 1874. Baxter's men closed the office in May so that no transaction

8. W. Drummond to C. Delano, February 24, 1874, in M849, Reel 3; A. K. Davis to Grant, February 27, 1874, J. L. Alcorn to C. Delano, March 4, 1874, B. K. Bruce to Z. Chandler, February 8, 1877, telegram of A. H. Mickie to Commissioner, 1891, all in M849, Reel 2.

9. K. Raynor (American and Spanish Commission) to Carl Schurz, June 19, 1877, in Appointments, Alabama.

of public business could take place.[10] This was the most drastic expression of how state politics affected federal positions.

Allegiance to party was not the only type of loyalty required of officeholders. To obtain federal appointment, all prospective public servants had to take the test oath, affirming not only future loyalty but past loyalty as well. The questionable manipulations by Alfred H. Carrigan illustrate all too clearly the lengths to which people would go to obtain office, the dubious nature of the oath-making process, and the motivations behind Andrew Johnson's distribution of the patronage. In 1865, Carrigan was tapped for a position with the local office in Washington, Arkansas. He had been a delegate to the secession convention and during the war had served in the Arkansas senate. His service in the rebel legislature meant that he could not swear to the test oath as it was printed; he boldly crossed out the parts of the pledge that said that he had never voluntarily borne arms against the United States or given aid to the enemy and that he had not held office in an enemy government or voluntarily supported any government hostile to the United States. He also added a line saying he would abide by the laws and proclamations made during the war relative to the emancipation of the slaves. His manipulations were useless, for his bond was not approved.[11]

The most radical part of "Radical" Reconstruction was participation of blacks in the political process, both as voters and as officeholders. Astute and practical politicians took notice of the potential strength of the black electorate and courted it, in part, by placing black men in various political offices. Not surprisingly, the southern public land states received several black officials, all of whom performed their duties as competently as their white colleagues did. At least one became embroiled in local politics.

10. Telegram of G. Denison and R. Edgerton to C. Delano, May 11, 1874, in Appointments, Arkansas.

11. Michael B. Dougan, *Confederate Arkansas: The People and Policies of a Frontier State in Wartime* (University, Ala., 1976), 47. Carrigan remembered secession in "Reminiscences of the Secession Convention," in Publications of the Arkansas Historical Association, I, 305–13. Official Bond of Carrigan, May 19, 1866 (written in 1865 and modified), in Appointments, Arkansas.

In March, 1873, Grant named James Somerville receiver in Mobile; he served in his position through Hayes's ascendancy. Spencer Terrell, another black man, discussed Somerville's attributes: "He is a good man and a true republican and more over he is strictly honest[. H]e is quite an ag[ree]able man and has a large family. . . . I am a Colered man and must tell you that the republican party in Ala. is composed mainly of Colered men and Mr. Sommerville is the only Colered man that we have in any influential possition whatever."[12]

The same year, Alabama received another black official when Grant nominated Peyton Finley for the position of receiver in Montgomery. In their recommendation, James T. Rapier and George Spencer called Finley "a prominent and leading colored man in our state." Finley was no political novice, for he was serving as county commissioner at the time of his nomination. Because he could not hold both offices, Finley gave up his job with the county to be receiver. In October, 1874, he decided to run for sheriff, so he tendered his resignation. By 1876, he was back in the land office and creating political havoc. One rival called him "an ignorant Negro," and the judge of probate court of Montgomery County said Finley was "wholly incompetent to discharge the duties of his office." Finley retained his post until 1877, when he sent his resignation to Secretary Carl Schurz. He never admitted whether political pressures had motivated him; he simply told Schurz that "biusiness interests in an other part of the State . . . require all my attention." His replacement was Paul Strobach, northerner, former state representative, Montgomery County sheriff, and later, unsuccessful candidate for a seat in Congress.[13]

The GLO employed two other black men in the South during the

12. Spencer Terrell to Z. Chandler, November 18, 1875, in Appointments, Alabama.

13. James T. Rapier and George Spencer to Grant, February 25, 1873, Rapier to Secretary of the Interior, May 3, 1873, Finley to Acting Secretary of the Interior, October, 1874, W. H. Hunter to GLO, April 23, 1876, extract of letter from W. H. Hunter to P. E. O'Connor, April 23, 1876, C. M. Buckley to Samuel Burdett, May 28, 1875, Finley to Schurz, 1877, Box 13, all in Appointments, Alabama. For information

Reconstruction years. Simon Jones, Johnson's only black appointee in the South's land offices, served as register in New Orleans for about six months in 1866. Grant named Robert Meacham register in Tallahassee in early 1871; he held his post for two years. Other black men either applied or were nominated for office but never served. Among them was P. B. S. Pinchback, to whom Grant offered the register's post in New Orleans in 1869.[14]

Just as politics played a crucial role in the appointments of registers and receivers, politics also provided the context in which local officers conducted business. Besides executing the land laws, the GLO's local agents had responsibilities for making reports, collecting monies, answering questions, and, in general, interpreting the laws. Not surprisingly, their actions did not always correspond to the intentions of the authors of the Southern Homestead Act. Irregularities surfaced continually.

Local officers were supposed to report business activity quarterly to the General Land Office and to forward any money they collected. Several were negligent in their duties, but the Jackson receivers were the most dilatory. From almost the time the office opened, the commissioner repeatedly asked them to forward their accounts. By 1869, frustration prompted the GLO to take the unprecedented step of preparing copies of accounts in Washington, sending them to Jackson, and having Receiver C. L. C. Cass sign and return them.

---

on Strobach, see Sarah Woolfolk Wiggins, *The Scalawag in Alabama Politics, 1865–1881* (University, Ala., 1977), 124–26, 139, 145–47, 149–50. See also Howard Rabinowitz, "Holland Thompson and Black Political Participation in Montgomery, Alabama," in Howard N. Rabinowitz (ed.), *Southern Black Leaders of the Reconstruction Era* (Urbana, 1982), 249–80.

14. Jones's appointment is hard to understand considering Johnson's views on race. No information can be found on Simon Jones. The others were Harry S. Harmon, Register, Gainesville; Robert J. Cromwell, Register, Gainesville; and Hannibal Carter, Register, Jackson. These facts were gleaned from the Appointment Papers in RG 48. See also William C. Harris, *The Day of the Carpetbagger: Republican Reconstruction in Mississippi* (Baton Rouge, 1979), 448–49. Carter was recommended by Mississippi Attorney General J. S. Morris, who would later argue in court for Carter and the state concerning the state Civil Rights Act of 1873, which Carter had coauthored.

The commissioner warned Cass that his lax performance would be reported to the secretary of the interior if he were not more diligent.

Even when Cass sent the returns on time, they were incomplete or full of errors. The receiver was scolded in typical fashion in May, 1872: "In the last returns received from your office . . . fully one third of the entries contain mistakes of one kind or another. Such mistakes it seems could not have been overlooked had the papers and abstracts been compared as you certify." The commissioner added, "The larger the number of errors made in the local office the more labor it imposes upon this office and on the local office in correcting said errors and in many instances it is a source of unnecessary annoyance and damage to the Homestead parties." In August, 1873, the commissioner compared the Jackson office to the others in the country: "In the hope that you will be more careful hereafter you are now informed that this office has more trouble in adjusting the accounts from Jackson Mississippi than any other Land Office in the Country." But nothing really changed, and Cass remained in office until 1876.[15]

The tendency of some officers to be negligent in forwarding reports manifested carelessness in other areas as well. A number of them were largely ignorant of General Land Office regulations and the provisions of the Southern Homestead Act in particular. Some charged wrong fees, allowed claims of land above the maximum acreage allowed by law, misread requirements, and generally did not observe the law's dictates.

Mischarging fees was the most common violation of the law. The Southern Homestead Act lowered to five dollars the ten-dollar entry fee of the 1862 Homestead Act and made it payable when the patent issued rather than at the time of entry. Commissions for registers and receivers remained at 2 percent. In late June, 1868, when the

15. GLO to C. L. C. Cass, October 9, 1869. See also letters to the Receiver of December 17, 1868, May 29, and June 30, 1869, GLO to Cass, March 28, 1870, GLO to Register and Receiver, May 23, 1872, GLO to Cass, August 13, 1873, GLO to Cass, October 19, 1874, all in Letters Sent. Lot M. Morrill, Secretary of the Treasury, to Zachariah Chandler, Secretary of the Interior, August 17, 1876, in Appointments, Mississippi, M849, Reel 2.

restriction limiting homesteads to eighty acres expired, the commissioner ruled that the five-dollar fee also expired. In other words, the fee was raised to ten dollars, now payable at the time of entry.[16]

Although there was room for doubt about a change in fees in 1868 before the commissioner ruled, the legislation was clear on fees before the acreage restriction was lifted. Nevertheless, E. C. Hatten and D. M. Bradford in Huntsville had to be reminded several times in June, 1867, about the proper fees and commissions. Officials in the newly opened Jackson office rejected applications that were not accompanied by a five-dollar fee, even though the law clearly stated that fees were payable only when the patent issued. The GLO scolded them and instructed the two to notify all those whose entries they had refused. When the policy changed in mid-1868, it apparently went unnoticed in Harrison, Arkansas, until 1873, for the old methods continued in force.[17] These examples do not indicate criminal malfeasance, simply ignorance of the law.

The homestead laws allowed the entry of fractional acreage above the legal maximum as long as the excess was paid in cash. The Southern Homestead Act set the maximum entry at 80 acres until June, 1868, and 160 acres after that. These amounts applied to so-called minimum land, or land that would normally sell for a cash price of $1.25 an acre. If land was classified as double minimum, or $2.50 an acre cash price, only half the maximum acreage could be claimed. That is, the maximum claim on double minimum land was 40 acres until June, 1868, or 80 acres after that. Before these acreage restrictions expired in 1868, any fraction over 80 acres minimum land constituted excess acreage; after that date, excess acreage was anything over 160 acres on minimum land.

16. The changes in fees can be followed in circulars the GLO issued entitled "The Manner of Proceeding to Obtain Title to Public Lands," September 17, 1867, August 30, 1872, and March 3, 1875, all in Circulars to State Land Officials, I (1821–72), II and III (1851–80), RG 49. The ruling for the change in fees in the South can be found in GLO to R&R of the southern states. For one example, see GLO to R&R, Huntsville, June 26, 1868, in Letters Sent.

17. GLO to R&R, Huntsville, several letters, June, 1867, in Letters Sent; Drummond to R&R, Harrison, March 26, 1873, GLO to R&R, Jackson, March 14, 1867, both in Division "A," Letters Sent.

Some officers did not understand this particular section of the law or chose to ignore it. For example, in late 1871 and early 1872, long after the maximum acreages had been raised, the Natchitoches officials repeatedly charged excess fees for any amount of land over 80 acres minimum land or 40 acres double minimum. Receiver William Hyatt of New Orleans charged for excesses over 80 acres after 1868 because his predecessors had done so. He explained that his earlier letters of inquiry concerning this matter had gone unanswered, so he assumed he was charging the correct fees.[18]

Local officers also violated the clause in the Southern Homestead Act that restricted claims to homesteads only. The Mobile officers allowed preemption claims, and New Orleans agents accepted cash for land sales. Huntsville's officials allowed graduation entries, and Jackson's register and receiver allowed land agents, for a fee, to answer inquiries directed to the land officers.[19]

Misinterpretation or misconstruction of the law or GLO regulations accounted for most of the irregularities in the southern public land offices. However, some local officials were downright incompetent. John Kirkwood, receiver in Little Rock, did not understand the basics of accounting; he "debited the Government with items which should have been placed to its credit, and vice versa, items to its credit which should have been debited." Other cases were even more serious. J. W. Gilbert, surveyor general of Florida, was an idiot. Congressman Josiah T. Walls and others wrote President Grant concerning Gilbert's mental qualifications: "The young man is a confirmed physical invalid, is weak-minded, and his natural strength of intellect is only a few degrees above idiocy, and the appointment will seem ludicrous in public estimation, and the public service will suffer in its dignity and efficiency." Gilbert had connections,

18. GLO to R&R, Natchitoches, November 27, 1871, GLO to Register, New Orleans, May 3, 1873, both in Division "A," Letters Sent; William Hyatt to Drummond, May 12, 1873, in MLR, K–49233.

19. GLO to Salmon Dutton, December 14, 1866, GLO to R&R, New Orleans, February 26, 1867, both in Letters Sent; Edward Hart to Wilson, March 7, 1867, in MLR, G–98810; GLO to R&R, New Orleans, March 19, 1867, GLO to R&R, Huntsville, January 17, 1870, both in Letters Sent; Curtis to Richard Kerr, June 13, 1873, Drummond to R&R, Jackson, June 24, 1873, both in Division "A," Letters Sent.

though; he was the son of the senator from Florida and served for over two years.[20]

Some of the irregularities, confusion, and incompetence can be attributed to the local officers holding political appointments; they had little, if any, expertise in federal land matters. But some of the problems went deeper. The very real and complex political entanglements in the states, coupled with the bureaucracy of the federal land office, provided a setting for less-than-honest people to use their position for personal or political gain. Corruption took many forms, but more often than not, local officers knowingly charged illegal fees; allowed timber to be stripped from the federal lands for a share of the proceeds; allowed fraudulent entries to skirt the homesteading-only provision of the law; accepted fees and contested claims for the purpose of displacing the freedmen; and gave certain "locating agents" exclusive rights to examine office records. Whatever the form, cheating and swindling benefited the dishonest while actual homesteaders, black and white, suffered the consequences.

Corruption haunted all three land office positions—register, receiver, and surveyor general. Although the actions of several of the surveyors were open to question in both Florida and Louisiana,[21] their dishonesty and favoritism pale in comparison with some of the charges leveled against the registers and receivers.

The register in Mobile was one of the first accused of dishonesty. Salmon Dutton, a native Vermonter who served for four years with a Vermont regiment during the war, came to the Mobile office in the summer of 1866 with recommendations from Alabama Governor

20. GLO to John Kirkwood, July 15, 1869, in Letters Sent; Josiah Walls, William Purman *et al.* to Grant, March 10, 1873, in Appointments, Florida.

21. See, for example, J. Wilson to M. L. Stearns, October 3, 1870, in SG Letters Sent; Stearns to Wilson, October 18, 1870, in SG Letters Received; Wilson to Stearns, October 26, 1870, in SG Letters Sent; Stearns to Wilson, November 17, 1870, in SG Letters Received; Wilson to Stearns, November 23, 1870, Drummond to E. W. Foster, August 17, 1871, both in SG Letters Sent; Foster to GLO, August 23, 1871, in SG Letters Received; GLO to Foster, August 30, 1871, in SG Letters Sent; J. Lynch to Grant, February 7, 9, 1871, L. A. Sheldon to Delano, March 7, 1871, Drummond to Delano, July 17, 1873, Foster to Delano, April 8, 1874, all in Appointments, Louisiana.

Lewis Parsons and Vermont's representatives and senators. In less than six months, homesteaders began bringing charges against him that would lead to his resignation in late 1868 while under federal investigation.

By the summer of 1868, business in the Mobile land office had gotten entirely out of hand, and several people called for an investigation. W. D. Mann of the Mobile *Daily Advertiser and Register* sent the GLO evidence against Dutton, and David Barton, a surveyor for forty years, complained to President Johnson and the GLO commissioner that business in the Mobile office was "conducted with extreme irregularity. The laws are violated, & the intrests of the Government are sacrificed habitually." He called for an investigation.[22]

The most complete indictment of Dutton's illegalities came from James Tharp, a clerk in the land office. Beginning his statement with a comment on Dutton's venality, Tharp said that he had known the register for two years "during which time he has kept a private office stiled the Land Office." For much of that time, Dutton worked without maps, records, and papers, allowing entries on lands of which he had no knowledge, and then not recording those applications on the books. As a result, two or more homesteaders often claimed the same plots. Dutton charged from twelve to fifty dollars in entry fees, and if the land had been previously claimed, he refused refunds. The register also allowed individuals to fill in fictitious names on certificates and claim the right to as many as ninety homesteads of eighty acres each. Tharp told of one person who paid Dutton $1,000 and then entered ninety-three homesteads for the purpose of obtaining the timber. Tharp concluded his scathing charges by reiterating that Dutton kept no public land office in Mobile, but instead traveled around collecting illegal fees and doing everything in his power to prevent the appointment of a receiver, in Tharp's words, "the better to continue [his] illegal proceedings."[23]

22. Commissioner Wilson sent the acting secretary the Mann papers on April 18, 1868. David Barton to Andrew Johnson, August 10, 1868, in Appointments, Alabama; the same letter to Wilson, in MLR, H–40332.

23. Sworn statement of James Tharp, August 14, 1868, J. Tharp to W. D. Mann, September 8, 1868, both in Appointments, Alabama.

Commissioner Joseph Wilson launched a special investigation of Dutton's activities in November, 1868, when he commissioned W. W. Curtis to look into the charges and secure a statement from the register. Curtis began accumulating more evidence almost immediately. Dutton must have known he was doomed; he sent his resignation to Washington on November 25, while the inquiry was still in progress.[24]

Curtis' investigation revealed the extent of Dutton's crimes. Tharp provided Curtis a list of almost five hundred tracts of land totaling approximately 34,580 acres, for which Dutton received illegal fees of between twelve and fifty dollars. Many of the entries were on private, school, or railroad lands, and therefore unavailable for homestead settlement. Curtis also discovered that Dutton had fraudulently allowed homestead entries for the express purpose of obtaining the timber from the lands. John H. Dent applied for land under the Southern Homestead Act—and entered six tracts in the names of six different people, paying twelve dollars each. He filed no affidavits and stated that some of the names he used were those of Negroes in his employ. Similarly, James and Tim Mahers claimed ninety-three tracts as homestead entries "for the purpose of cutting & taking off the timber." They paid Dutton's twelve-dollar asking fee for each tract as well as "a large amount of money" to remove the timber and sell it for their own benefit. They never had any intention "of settling themselves or others upon the land."[25]

Curtis completed his investigation and filed his report on December 4. He stated at the outset that what he had found was "but a small part of what might be, with further time, collected respecting the irregularities of the Register." He then summarized Dutton's wrongdoing. The first transgression was acting without a receiver,

24. Wilson to Secretary Browning, November 5, 1868, copy of instructions to W. W. Curtis from Wilson, November 9, 1868, Salmon Dutton to Wilson, November 25, 1868, all in Appointments, Alabama.

25. Affidavit of D. Barton and J. Tharp, November 25, 1868, list of depredations on public lands reported by G. Gregg, statement of D. M. N. Ross concerning John H. Dent, November 20, 1868, affidavit of David Barton, November 25, 1868, concerning the Mahers' claim, all in Appointments, Alabama.

accepting homestead applications and giving certificates under his signature only. Second, he overcharged fees. Third, he sold lands as cash entries for the minimum price of $1.25 an acre. Fourth, he accepted money from trespassers upon the public lands and then kept it. Fifth, he kept no record of any of his transactions. Sixth, most of the transactions were made "with crafty and designing men who acted with the full intent of defrauding the government," although there were a "great many poor men, white and colored," who "were induced to make applications for Homesteads and who paid the excessive fees under the belief that the whole procedure was legal." Curtis could not even estimate the financial extent of the fraud. The new receiver believed that people had paid Dutton between thirty and forty thousand dollars, and that sum did not include the private sales or homestead fees. Nor could Curtis determine the amount of illegal timber that had been cut. He did say, accusingly, that the lands had been converted into "turpentine orchards," and he recommended legislation to prevent the tapping of the trees on the public lands.

Dutton refused to make any written statements, although he did tell the investigator that he was trying to provide homes for the freedmen. Curtis rejected this claim, believing that it was "impossible that [Dutton] could have been thus decieved." Furthermore, the men who made fraudulent applications were not the type "to take an active interest in behalf of freedmen." Curtis would not go so far as to blame Dutton; he was convinced that the unfortunate officer, who had been "a good soldier during the late war," had come under the dastardly influences of "bad men" who wished to use him for their own benefit. Curtis' concluding words spoke forcefully to the problem of unqualified public land officers: he recommended that the GLO "send some person conversant with the land system" to Mobile to get the office in order and "to educate the new officers in the details of their official duties."[26]

26. Report on investigation of S. Dutton to J. Wilson from W. W. Curtis, December 4, 1868, in Appointments, Alabama. See also William Howard to Wilson, January 30, 1869, in MLR, H–53752, for the dollar estimates of fraud.

Dutton's is not the only example of illegality. Abraham Edwards in Montgomery charged illegal fees and, contrary to regulations, collected two dollars every time he provided someone with information. George Denison and Rollins Edgerton in Little Rock did so as well, but with a flair for formality: they printed notices that said they were charging for information. The last line of the notice read, "To receive attention, the amount necessary will be ———." For example, when D. H. Rousseau inquired about certain land, he received "official" notice that the information would cost him one hundred dollars. The Camden, Arkansas, office began business under a similar dark cloud; Register Darius S. Griffin was suspended about nine months after his appointment for illegally charging $2.50 for public information.[27]

The Harrison, Arkansas, office opened rather inauspiciously as well. The first register, E. J. Rhodes, faced charges of speculation and collusion soon after he assumed his duties, but he believed that the allegations were brought by those who were politically jealous of his position. His accuser held a large amount of land, worked by tenants, and Rhodes was convinced that this schemer wanted the government job so he could acquire clear title to his holdings. Senator Powell Clayton called for Rhodes's removal. Rhodes and his receiver, John Torrence, replied to each charge, and Commissioner

27. GLO to R&R, Montgomery, December 10, 1868, in Letters Sent; W. W. Dobson to Wilson, December 11, 1868, in MLR, H–50021; A. Edwards to Wilson, December 22, 1868, in MLR, H–50431; GLO to Edwards, January 5, 1869, in Letters Sent. Edwards' successor, Pelham J. Anderson, was also accused of overcharging. His explanation suited the GLO, for he served several terms. Samuel E. Wallace to Interior, November 4, 1870 (referred to R&R on November 16), in MLR, I–23272; Anderson to Wilson, December 8, 1870, in MLR, I–27735; GLO to Anderson, December 16, 1870, in Letters Sent; D. H. Rousseau to Drummond, September 16, 1872, in MLR, K–17339. The printed notice is dated July 26, 1870. Willis Drummond to Delano, November 3, 1871, in Appointments, Arkansas. Enclosed is a letter of attorneys Bradley and Rousseau, September 12, 1871, requesting the public information. Griffin wrote the commissioner on February 26, 1872 (I–84422), objecting to his manner of removal, stating he had not been tried and furthermore was not guilty. The postmaster at Washington, Arkansas, accused James Torrans, Johnson's receiver, of exaggerating his account for postage stamps in order to defraud the government. See GLO to J. Torrans, September 2, 1868, in Letters Sent. Charges were also leveled against A. A. Tufts and S. W. Mallory at Camden in 1877, but it appears that they were brought on by a jealous office-seeker. See Appointments, Arkansas, Tufts-Mallory file.

Willis Drummond did not proceed with removal. Whether or not the two broke the law is unclear; it is more likely that the charges actually were politically motivated. This is corroborated by evidence from a petition submitted to Senator Clayton that accused Rhodes and Torrence of "open hostility towards the State and National Administrations." It went on to say that "their office is the nightly rendevous of men who are the tools of the KuKlux Democracy, in the pay of the enemies of the Republican party and the President of the United States for the purpose of defeating that party." It is not without significance that among the petitioners were Rhodes's original accuser and the next receiver.[28]

In early 1876, scandal once again brought attention to the Harrison office when officers J. M. Doubleday and A. Prather faced allegations of fraud and deceit. Several homestead parties accused the officials of allowing claims on lands that had been claimed previously. One disgruntled man asked Doubleday who rightfully owned the land, to which the register baldly replied, "The man who gives the most money will get it." Another homesteader, who could not afford to pay the fees to legitimize her claim, sold her land to Prather at his suggestion, and she and her son then became tenants on the same tract she had originally desired to own. About two months later, someone tried to cover up these irregularities, but the woman came forward and attested to the authenticity of the facts in the case, and it was brought to light that Prather's intention was to "mak[e] a little money."[29]

In their defense the register and receiver protested that the charges against them were politically motivated, that the people

28. E. J. Rhodes to Secretary of the Interior, September 22, 1871, in Appointments, Arkansas; G. W. M. Reed to GLO, December 28, 1871, in MLR, I–76510; affidavit of John C. Phillips, June 6, 1872, J. M. Johnson to P. Clayton, August 21, 1872, Rhodes to Commissioner, September 9, 1872, Rhodes and Torrence to Commissioner, September 12, 1872, Drummond to Delano, September 28, 1872, petition to Clayton, n.d., all in Appointments, Arkansas.

29. Affidavit of C. W. Mitchell, January 13, 1876, affidavit of William F. Berry, January 19, 1876, affidavit of Susan Brewer, March 6, 1876, affidavit of John M. Brewer, March 6, 1876, affidavit of S. Dial, May 6, 1876, affidavits of Susan Brewer and J. M. Brewer, May 15, 1876, all in Appointments, Arkansas. For other charges, see John Berry to Commissioner, March 15, 1876, in Appointments, Arkansas.

who had purportedly been cheated were actually dupes of men who were trying to oust Doubleday and Prather from office. As the heat on them increased in the fall, Prather appealed to President Grant, claiming he was the object of political manipulations. Prather eventually resigned, and Doubleday followed him out less than a year later.

It is unclear why they voluntarily left office; perhaps the political situation had become too uncomfortable, at least for Prather. Evidence strongly suggests that several men in north Arkansas were displeased with the federal appointments and wished to replace them. In fact, the very person who earlier accused Rhodes of wrongdoing loomed behind some of the plottings in 1876 and 1877. The last word came from Commissioner J. A. Williamson, who told his boss, Secretary Schurz, in March, 1878, that the register and receiver had "fully replied" to the allegations against them and that the investigation should be stopped, since Prather had already resigned.[30]

In Florida, charges mounted against A. B. Stonelake, the first register appointed after the war. He practiced favoritism, but more serious, he swindled several hundred freedmen out of their life savings while repeatedly claiming he was trying to help them. Stonelake worked out an arrangement with Freedmen's Bureau Commissioner O. O. Howard to secure "locating agents" to survey lands for freedmen, without cost to them. A group of about three hundred former slaves from South Carolina decided to take advantage of the homestead laws and migrate to New Smyrna, Florida. General Ralph Ely, formerly in South Carolina with the Freedmen's Bureau, collected about six hundred dollars from the freedmen and sent the required fees to Stonelake. The register allowed Ely to pencil upon

30. Doubleday to GLO, April 29, 1876, A. Prather to Commissioner, October 2, 1876, Prather to Grant, October 2, 1876, Dorsey to Williamson, October 9, 1876, and Prather to Dorsey, October 14, 1876, Prather's letter of resignation to Hayes, dated January 1877 (this must be 1878, for Hayes was not yet in office), and Doubleday's letter of resignation to Hayes, December 10, 1878, William Keener to C. Schurz, July 26, 1877, Prather to Dorsey, October 28, 1877, Williamson to Schurz, March 9, 1878, all in Appointments, Arkansas.

the plats the lands he wished to take. Stonelake believed the group would select their lots and make their applications officially when they arrived at New Smyrna.

In the meantime, a problem originating in Washington complicated matters. The GLO did not allow business in old districts until they were officially consolidated with another district. Because the old St. Augustine district, where New Smyrna was located, had not yet been consolidated with Tallahassee, the GLO prohibited Stonelake from allowing entry of the freedmen's lands. Ely demanded refund of the six hundred dollars. Stonelake refused because, he said, the freedmen had paid the fees with the intent of homesteading. Returning the money amounted to swindling the freedmen because the would-be settlers had already left South Carolina. Stonelake explained, "The freedmen . . . were not brought to Florida at Government expense, to have their money returned after their arrival, but to enter land under the Homestead Law." Here the story becomes even more confused, because the register apparently contradicted himself. Along with the fees, Ely had also sent applications, but Stonelake refused to receive them because lands in the St. Augustine district were not yet subject to entry. Apparently, the fees were legal but applications were not.

An undisclosed source informed Howard of the problems associated with the unconsolidated districts and at the same time exposed Stonelake for collecting and holding "hundreds if not thousands of dollars [taken] illegally from the negroes." The receiver in Tallahassee, Ozias Morgan, believed that the register's actions were not above suspicion, because he discovered that some sort of deal had been negotiated between Ely and Stonelake without any consideration for the interests of the freedmen. Morgan based his assertions on the fact that Stonelake returned all affidavits in his possession for correction except the three hundred that Ely had filed.

It was at this point that the GLO confronted Stonelake, asking him for a full report. Washington, disturbed by the use of the locating agents in Florida and elsewhere, advised the register that the GLO recognized no such officers. However, the GLO conceded that if such agents were useful to the freedmen, the GLO had no problem with them, but the arrangements must be entirely between the Freedmen's Bureau and its agents. In June, 1867, Stonelake offered an extensive defense of his actions. He knew firsthand that some people placed serious obstacles in the way of the freedmen's obtaining land, including everything from overcharging surveyors' fees to placing the hapless freedmen on lands far away from those they wanted—usually in the middle of a swamp. Stonelake traveled about his district to warn them, instructing the freedmen in churches and other places about the Southern Homestead Act. But he could do nothing about the surveyors, so he had approached Howard about using Freedmen's Bureau agents to help. The register said he believed that his office had treated all parties fairly and that it had used all money as had been intended. The commissioner remained unconvinced, and Stonelake resigned in September.[31]

Louisiana has always been perceived as politically corrupt, but other southern and northern states also operated unethically during Reconstruction. It is somewhat difficult to ascertain the extent of fraud because, as in other states, accusations were often too intimately tied to political enmity. For example, political squabbling began in Natchitoches in 1869 when Grant named Henry C. Myers register. One person claimed Myers was a Democrat, but several citizens of Natchitoches defended him as "a good Republican" and "competent officer." Nevertheless, in late 1871, in spite of the plead-

31. A. B. Stonelake to Wilson, February 21, 1867, in MLR, G–99381; Stonelake to Wilson, June 27, 1867, in MLR, H–7941; O. O. Howard to Wilson, May 15, 1867, in MLR, H–3592; O. Morgan to Wilson, May 30, 1867, in MLR, H–6978; GLO to R&R, June 20, 1867, in Letters Sent; Stonelake to Wilson, June 27, 1867, in MLR, H–7941; Morgan to Wilson, October 18, 1867, forwarding Ely's letter of the 15th, in MLR, H–15634. There are accounts of the New Smyrna colony in two works, Richardson, *The Negro in the Reconstruction of Florida*, 74–75, and Oubre, *Forty Acres*, 143–47. Besides this swindling of the freedmen, there were other charges against Stonelake. For example, he reputedly disallowed a claim so that it could go to a former Confederate, and this during the six-month exclusionary period. See J. P. Johnson to Commissioner, April 28, 1866, in MLR, G–86023; Johnson to Wilson, February 3, 1867, in MLR, G–96274. A petition from citizens of Palatka, Florida, June 25, 1867, in MLR, H–7816, accused Stonelake of allowing homestead entries on state and swamp and overflowed lands, ignoring the persons who owned these already.

ing of Governor Henry Clay Warmoth and Senator J. R. West, Myers was suspended for overcharging, favoritism to political friends, too many absences, and incompetence. In the end, the allegations proved to be politically motivated, for a congressional committee exploring the conditions in the South in 1875 concluded that it could not justify charges against Myers and that the White League of Louisiana had harassed him.[32]

A. W. Faulkner, the first register in Monroe, became innocently embroiled in a fraudulent insurance scheme. An agent of a Hartford, Connecticut, firm, Faulkner got caught in the middle of a plan to defraud the company. The guilty parties forged names to a policy so that they could collect money upon the "death" of one of the plotters. The incident appeared in most of the conservative New Orleans papers, but Faulkner was exonerated and later elected to the Louisiana Legislature.[33]

Officers in the largest city in Louisiana did not escape the opportunities for corruption that came with the power of office. Charles Barnard and William H. Hyatt, register and receiver in New Orleans, could not explain satisfactorily allegations of overcharging fees or collecting money for delivering patents. Especially damning, they denied such charges when the evidence clearly demonstrated fraud. Although prominent Republicans claimed that the complaints were politically motivated, GLO Commissioner Willis Drummond recommended the officers' removal because they had not answered all charges as fully as possible. They received their notices in May, 1873.[34]

32. H. C. Myers to A. Johnson, August 18, 1868, J. O. Orsborn to William P. Kellogg, March 29, 1872, petition of Republicans of Natchitoches Parish to Grant, n.d. [August, 1872], Warmoth endorsement, November 11, 1871, J. R. West to Drummond, November 13, 1871, petition by six citizens against Myers, September 20, 1871, (letter in report of F. Stiles, August 7, 1876), *House Reports, Condition of the South*, 43rd Cong., 2nd Sess., No. 261, pp. 15–16, all in Appointments, Louisiana.

33. A. W. Faulkner to Wilson, July 17, 1869, in MLR, H–71067. This document contains several enclosures, including clippings from the New Orleans *Times*, April 4, 1869, and the New Orleans *Crescent*, April 6, 1869.

34. J. L. Bradford to R. H. Bradford, January 21, 1872, affidavit of Barnard and Hyatt, February 16, 1872, Francis J. Herron (Secretary of State) to Drummond, February 21, 1872, affidavit of Barnard and Hyatt, n.d., Hyatt affidavit to Drummond,

"Swindling concerns," "private office"—these and countless other phrases described illegal or irregular actions at the southern public land offices. Overcharging fees, allowing timber depredations, depositing fees in their own pockets, recording fictitious entries for fraudulent purposes, using their offices to extort money from the freedmen, favoring certain agents and business acquaintances for personal gain: the registers, receivers, and surveyors general practiced these and other illegal activities in their official capacities. Some did it for their own profit; others for friends; still others for party. Resignation did not necessarily imply guilt; sometimes it meant that political enemies had won the day, at least in removing their foes from office. Curiously enough, resignation meant the end of the road for any further investigation. None of the southern land officers was ever prosecuted for his offenses.

Southern officeholders did not have a monopoly on corruption and ignorance. Scandal reached from the local levels all the way up to the higher ranks of Grant's administration. What makes these aberrations so central in the South was their effect on homesteading. Homesteaders themselves brought many of the charges to the attention of the General Land Office. When registers and receivers were not performing their jobs, when the local office had only one of the two required officers, or when the appointee interfered with homesteading, it was the homesteader who suffered.[35] Getting down to business is a story of its own, but more important, the reason to get to work was to open the public lands in the South to settlement. The fact that so many obstacles blocked the way exacerbated the already overwhelming hardships of beginning a new life.

April 3, 1872, affidavit of James L. Bradford, June 18, 1872, Robert H. and J. L. Bradford to Commissioner, March 19, 1873, Drummond to Delano, April 1, 1873, all in Appointments, Louisiana.

35. Appendix B shows the annual homestead figures for each state. There is a positive correlation between conditions in the local office at a particular time and the decline in the number of homestead applications.

III

Getting and Keeping the Land

The supporters of the Southern Homestead Act expected southern homesteaders, principally the landless former slaves, to gain an economic foundation for themselves by becoming individual landholders, thereby helping eventually to transform the old plantation South into a section of small farms. More to the point, because it restricted the public lands solely to homesteading, the act embodied the most extravagant statement of the agrarian myth, the dream of a nation of farmers. Practical factors and realities, however, had their ways of interfering with that dream. Time and time again, homesteaders ran into obstacles that revealed the tenuous foundations of the policy. Their stories—their problems, disappointments, frustrations, accomplishments—illustrate vividly how the Southern Homestead Act usually worked in the Louisiana swamps, in the northern Mississippi forests, on the Florida beaches, in the Arkansas hills, and along the Alabama coast.

When they seceded from the Union, the southern public land states appropriated the public domain within their borders, most simply by passing legislation seizing federal property. Alabama went so far as to order a registration of lands and to adopt the federal land system. Indeed, its secession convention went further: it provided for the nation's first homestead law. All of the seceded states jealously guarded these new resources; none made any effort to cede their public lands to the Confederate government. The Confederate Congress, however, passed a resolution asking the states to cede as much of the domain as might be valuable for its timber to aid in "naval or other purposes of public concern."[1] Some people took out claims, or entered lands, in the Confederate states, but after the war, the United States refused to recognize them. For all practical purposes, the land offices in the southern land states remained closed during the war.

After the war, white southern landowners were apprehensive about the future, especially the uncertain new relationships between former master and former slave that emancipation promised. Perhaps even more than the social concerns, the economic questions needed immediate answers. Who would work the plantation lands? Would the freedmen leave their old homes? How would any labor force be paid? Most crucially, white landowners were convinced that they did not know how to work free labor. Believing that blacks would leave the land to demonstrate their liberty, whites feared a labor shortage, and any offer of free land only exacerbated these concerns. So, even before the Southern Homestead Act passed, and perhaps surprisingly because of their recent bitter defeat, white southerners began recruiting settlers from outside the South.[2] They launched an active program, organizing homestead associations and other private agencies. Some individuals saw lucrative possibilities and set up shop to aid potential settlers, for a fee, to locate homesteads.

In September of 1865, promoters organized the Arkansas Immigrant Aid Society. Its slate of officers showed that it was an ambitious organization. Arkansas' secretary of state, Robert J. T. White, was named president. Governor Isaac Murphy and Senator Powell Clayton were among the vice-presidents. To help accomplish

1. May Spencer Ringold, *The Role of the State Legislatures in the Confederacy* (Athens, Ga., 1966), 3; Walter L. Fleming, *Civil War and Reconstruction in Alabama* (1905; rpr. Gloucester, Mass., 1949), 50, 258; Dougan, *Confederate Arkansas*, 64; John E. Johns, *Florida During the Civil War* (Gainesville, 1963), 99, 106; John K. Bettersworth, *Confederate Mississippi* (1943; rpr. Philadelphia, 1978), 11; *Senate Documents, Journal of the Congress of the Confederate States of America, 1861–1865*, 58th Cong., 2nd Sess., No. 234, pp. 80, 110, 144–45, 151.

2. Eric Foner has explored the relationship between immigration to the South and black landownership in *Nothing But Freedom*, 47–48.

its grand design of attracting immigrants, the society called for the establishment of agencies in such places as New York, Philadelphia, and New Orleans.[3]

Florida had a similar organization, the Southern Land and Immigration Company, which received its charter from the Florida Legislature; Governor David Walker was the president. The agency intended to spend at least half a million dollars to attract settlers. Walker appointed Tallahassee Register A. B. Stonelake as a delegate to the Planters' Convention in Monticello, Florida, in August, 1867, to help promote immigration to Florida. Within a short time, Stonelake resigned his post in Tallahassee after other schemes linked him directly with fraud. But resignation from his official position did not mean the end of his land business, for almost immediately he went to New York City and established the American Homestead Land and Immigration Office at 66 Broadway. The former register believed that his out-of-state services could be useful because everyone who wanted land could not afford to go to Florida to get it. Stonelake advertised extensively, even in Europe, and claimed immediate success: less than a week after the first advertising circular went out, he received applications for thirty homesteads.[4]

Besides these organizations, established to attract settlers to private and public lands, certain individuals, billing themselves as locating or real estate agents, aided actual settlement. In their message and methods, these men heralded the advent of the New South. A circular entitled "Alabama Reconstructed!," issued at the end of 1867 by two locating agents, contained all the ingredients preachers of the New South gospel would use in their propaganda twenty years later. In their words, "Investments can be made within the next twelve months, that from three to five years will advance as

3. Constitution of the Arkansas Immigrant Aid Society, enclosed in a letter of W. D. Snow, clipped from a Little Rock newspaper, in Appointments, Arkansas.

4. Mobile *Daily Advertiser and Register*, May 30, 1867; Stonelake to Wilson, July 31, 1867, in MLR, H–10635; Stonelake to Wilson, September 25, 1867, in MLR, H–14106. He enclosed two circulars advertising his services. He signed the circulars, "Late Register of U.S. Lands in Florida."

many hundred per cent. Vast beds of Iron, Coal, Copper and Lead, besides Gold and Silver, as well as Marble stone, Soapstone, Flagstone, Roofing Slate, Limestone, in abundance and of the finest quality, Porcelain Clay, besides Salt, Lignite and Marl are found in quantities inexhaustible, and in quality the very best." They went on to outline various other products, such as petroleum and timber, that were certain to attract capital to the state. For those wanting to farm but skeptical about single-crop agriculture, these perspicacious men announced that Alabama did not live by cotton alone: wheat could be grown profitably in the northern part of the state, and corn and other cereals could be produced anywhere. To quiet sectional animosities and to reassure potential settlers that their investments were safe, they pointedly denied that northern men were unwelcome. Prejudice and bitterness, these promoters wrote, "must give way or be crushed beneath the iron tread of genuine progress and universal justice."[5]

It is impossible to measure the extent of the appeal of these heralds, but if letters from the North and West requesting information are any indication, then the campaign showed promise. From everywhere, applicants specifically asked about property in the southern public land states. Most seemed to have their eyes on Florida; interest in settlement and development there existed long before the end of Reconstruction. The inquiries seem endless, but a few examples are typical. George Scott, of Baltimore, wanted to settle near St. Augustine in February, 1867. The location was not as important as the quality of the land. He complained, "At all events we wish to go where the soil is good [,] as we have had, and seen enough of working poor land." Reports of Florida's "climate, soil, timber, fruits, lakes" tempted Edward B. Clark and his friends from Philadelphia, "all young, active men, and ready for real *working* enterprise," but they wanted more information before they set out to make "a home in the wilds of a new state." Many land seekers had served in the South during the war and liked what they saw. A.

5. Circular, "Alabama Reconstructed!," December 27, 1867, by John T. Morgan and W. H. F. Randall, in MLR, H–20794.

Patten, a dental surgeon from Biddeford, Maine, was one of these and wished to move to Florida with his brother to raise cotton and sugar.[6]

Not all the requests for information came from the northern states; southerners from states with no more public lands showed interest, too. James Hall and other planters near Memphis desired farms in western Arkansas, and Lieutenant A. W. Corliss, of Charleston, wanted property in Alabama. Some people from southern states with public lands wished to move to another southern public land state. For example, William Fryer, of New Orleans, wanted to settle in the Mobile district, and J. M. Dickerson, of Newtonville, Mississippi, wanted to homestead in Calcasieu Parish in southwestern Louisiana.[7]

Many would-be settlers quickly discovered that homesteading made more taxing demands than anticipated. Long distances to the local office all too often created initial inconveniences. The law required that people claim their lands in person at the land office or, if that was impossible, before the clerk of the court of the county where the plot was located. A random study of the entry papers for a state like Mississippi, which had only one office, in Jackson, proves that most entries were in fact made before a county clerk.[8]

Homesteaders in sparsely settled Florida probably had the greatest difficulty with the location of land offices and county clerks. George Alden, who was associated with the troubled colony at New Smyrna, complained that Tallahassee, thirty-five miles away, was too far away to reach economically. As deputy collector of customs, Alden wanted permission to do the official land business for the area. If New Smyrna was too far from Tallahassee, then the settlers

6. An examination of the Registers of Letters Received at the GLO between 1866 and 1876 reveals the extent of the inquiries. George Scott to Commissioner, February 6, 1867, in MLR, G–96524; Edward B. Clark to Commissioner, April 16, 1867, in MLR, H–1458; A. Patten to Commissioner, May 30, 1867, in MLR, H–4775.

7. James Hall to Wilson, February 25, 1870, in MLR, H–93635; A. W. Corliss to Wilson, May 29, 1870, in MLR, I–3862; William K. F. Fryer to Edmunds, December 1, 1866, in MLR, G–91652; J. M. Dickerson to Edmunds, July 2, 1866, in MLR, G–82067.

8. The homestead papers are kept at the Federal Records Center, Suitland, Md. See Appendix A for more on the Mississippi study.

in Dade County in southern Florida must have felt they were in a foreign land. Horace Porter suggested that a new office be opened in that part of the state because a trip to Gainesville, where the local office had been moved, involved a journey of a thousand miles. His request went unheeded.[9]

If an applicant surmounted the problem of distance to the district office, he was likely to discover a host of other roadblocks to pass prior to completing his claim. Before proceeding with the business of making a home, settlers often had to establish their rightful claims to a plot. They frequently could not determine the location of the available public lands, partly because of incomplete and unsatisfactory record keeping by the local officers, partly because it was virtually impossible to keep precise maps of the public lands. Their status changed from day to day. The tract books and the township plats together were the only accurate sources—and those depended on diligent officers. The General Land Office recognized this problem, but found no satisfactory solution. "The status of any tract of public land," the commissioner explained, "is liable at any moment to change by its desposal, or by withdrawal from market [;] consequently the maps so furnished would be a continual source of error creating expense and embarrasment instead of reliable information for the parties consulting them."[10]

The difficulty of finding available public lands often led to trouble for homesteaders. Some hopeful settlers inadvertently established themselves on the wrong tracts, resulting in conflicts once their

9. George J. Alden to Drummond, August 5, 1871, in MLR, I–59652; Horace P. Porter to Commissioner, October 20, 1873, in MLR, K–74168. The route from Dade County took travelers from Biscayne Bay to Key West, northward to Cedar Keys, and thence to Gainesville.

10. GLO to R&R, Montgomery, December 22, 1868, in Letters Sent. The commissioner touched upon a problem for the researcher, too. There is no ready way to determine where the southern public lands were. The only way to do so would be to freeze a moment in time and construct a map from the tract books and township plats. Such a process would undoubtedly be tedious, but in this age of computer technology, it seems that it might be possible. There is at least one map, called "Langtree's New Sectional Map of the State of Arkansas," drawn in 1866 and located in the Geography and Map Division of the Library of Congress, showing the location of the public lands in Arkansas.

errors were discovered. C. K. Harney, who was barely literate, was complying with the law "in good Faith" in order to secure title to his land near Hot Springs, Arkansas. When he applied for his plot, there was no county surveyor to run out the lines of his claim, the original markings having been destroyed by fire. He reasoned that "the county was too poor too pay eny body." Later, Harney himself hired a surveyor, who discovered the worst: the land Harney had settled on was not the land he had claimed on the tract books. Harney even offered to pay the minimum price to get it.[11]

Another issue closely related to determining the whereabouts of the public lands was ascertaining which were the reserved lands—those sections of public lands that had been set aside for specific purposes and where homesteading was prohibited. These restrictions were often buried in obscure antebellum enactments and frequently had been ignored by land officers in previous decades. The southern public land states had several categories of reserved lands. The bulk were either swamp and "overflow" lands or railroad grants, together totaling approximately 35 million acres.[12] The proceeds from the sales of these lands would go toward the reclamation of the swamplands and the building of railroads. The status of the reserved lands varied from time to time, and this ever-changing classification exacerbated the problems created by inadequate records. In addition, local officers, although restricted by the law, allowed settlers to homestead on the reserved lands, thereby creating additional difficulties, not only for the GLO, but more important, for the actual settlers who would find out too late that they had begun farms on lands from which they would soon be evicted.

Even if public lands were properly located, the homesteading process—known as settlement and cultivation—provided enough obstacles to defeat most settlers. Depending on an infinite variety of circumstances, the claimants would either fulfill the requirements and gain title to the land or pack up and move on. When

11. C. K. Harney to Commissioner, October 5, 1874, in MLR, L–22479.
12. Compiled from Department of the Interior, General Land Office, *Annual Report of the Commissioner of the General Land Office* (1866), 73, 151–52.

homesteaders failed to acquire title, GLO regulations recognized only two scenarios—abandonment and voluntary relinquishment. Abandonment, for all practical purposes, meant deserting a claim. It differed from relinquishment in that it entailed no positive return of the land to the government by the settler. Practically, abandoning a plot tied it up for quite some time in bureaucratic entanglements, especially if someone else wanted the land, since the first claimant retained various legal rights until hearings could be held and the claim officially given up. From a public policy standpoint, contesting an abandoned claim may have made good sense, but proving abandonment was complicated and troublesome, even though the law stated that absences from a homestead for more than six months constituted abandonment.

The records of the General Land Office contain numerous examples of abandoned homestead claims. Many times, the deserting party could not be located for the required hearings, even after due notice had been published in the local papers. In such cases, the land reverted to the government. If the original homesteader could be found, the register and receiver held hearings and issued an opinion; the commissioner of the GLO would then make a final ruling. Two different cases illustrate the difficulties of such rulings.

In 1872, someone contested John B. Gilliam's homestead in the Huntsville district because he was not on it. Gilliam claimed he had left his land for six months due to illness in his family, but he had entrusted his personal belongings and livestock to his father, who remained behind. These signs of settlement, coupled with his stated intention to return to his plot, persuaded the GLO to allow Gilliam to retain his homestead claim. Thomas W. Winstead, of Mississippi, was not so fortunate. He had "bartered away and alienated a portion" of his entry to Fred Harrison, "a colored man," for a price. The commissioner ruled that this action amounted to abandonment, and he held Winstead's entry for cancellation.[13]

Sometimes claiming public lands for homesteads involved ob-

13. GLO to R&R, Huntsville, March 22, 1871, GLO to R&R, Jackson, July 15, 1875, both in Letters Sent.

vious fraud. The case of Charvey Barbe, of Lake Charles, Louisiana, demonstrates not only the methods by which some people deceived the General Land Office and the actual settler, but the crimes they would commit to do it. Barbe made inquiries about acquiring public land as early as March, 1868, and applied for a homestead in February the following year. In May, 1872, he decided to take advantage of the commutation clause of the law, which allowed settlers to pay for their claims after only a six-month required residency. The GLO approved the plot for patenting in July, which means that Barbe had sworn that he had fulfilled his obligations.[14] Soon thereafter, J. B. Bideaux and Severine Sallier charged Barbe with perjury, alleging Barbe did not live on the property, because they were living on it. Barbe, who was postmaster in Lake Charles, had promised Bideaux he would claim the land for him. Instead, Barbe applied in his own name and fled the parish. No one knew his whereabouts.

Bideaux and Sallier were not satisfied with a mere complaint; they helped secure an indictment for perjury in April, 1873. It asserted that Barbe had not settled on the land, did not occupy it at the time he said he did, never lived on it, and did not have acreage fenced off or under cultivation—all of which he had sworn in the oath. A grand jury then charged Barbe with perjury.[15]

The GLO suspended patenting, pending the outcome of the case. A state court sustained Barbe's plea, but the prosecution decided to take the charges to federal court in New Orleans, and they requested further suspensions from the General Land Office. By May, 1874, the verdict was still undecided, and the final disposition is unknown. Barbe was a prominent resident and officeholder in Lake

14. C. Barbe to Commissioner, March 14, 1868, in MLR, H–27977; Barbe to Commissioner, January 25, 1871, in MLR, I–34155; Drummond to C. B. Darrall, February 5, 1873, in Division "C," Letters Sent to Members of Congress, RG 49.

15. R. H. and J. L. Bradford to Commissioner, February 12, 1873, in MLR, K–35669, with enclosure. Louis Palms to Robert Bradford, February 12, 1873, R. H. and J. L. Bradford to Commissioner, February 24, 1873, both in MLR, K–36974, with the following enclosures: affidavit of J. B. Bideaux, December 30, 1872, affidavits of John B. Bideaux and Severine Sallier, April 14, 1873, affidavit of W. H. Kirkman, February 14, 1873, indictment of Charvey Barbe for perjury, April, 1873.

Charles. Several of the city's distinguished families lined up on one side or the other; Sallier, Kirkman, Ryan, and Barbe had turned the matter into a noteworthy issue. Before it was over, Barbe had enlisted Congressman C. B. Darrall to help him secure his patent.[16]

Fraud led frequently to the cancellation of homesteads, but more often, a claim would be canceled because two people demanded title to the same plot. Careless bookkeeping, obliterated surveys, local officers' incompetence or malfeasance, all increased the likelihood that two people would enter the same piece of land. The usual case involved squatters who had established residency and later discovered that they were living on federal lands that had been claimed legally by someone else. Squatting, or preemption, was illegal in the South from 1866 to 1876. But the GLO was not hardhearted: the commissioner adopted the policy of recognizing prior improvements because, in the GLO's oft-repeated phrase, "it is not the policy of the System to allow one man to appropriate for himself the improvements resulting from the labor of another." If there was some legitimate reason for official proceedings, the local officers conducted hearings, but the GLO became increasingly intolerant of cases "based merely upon alleged prior settlement, cultivation, or improvement"[17] and began canceling entries that did not follow the letter of the law.

The charges that Joseph G. Wilson brought against William E. Smith in 1871 in the Camden district illustrate not only the government's position but also the lengths to which settlers would go to substantiate their claims. William Smith had entered a plot in November, 1869. Within six months, he had cleared an old field, sown a small quantity of oats, and repaired an old fence, but he failed to move onto the land until February, 1871, shortly *after*

16. Curtis to Bradfords, March 8, 1873, in M25, Reel 114; Curtis to Bradfords, May 10, 1873, in M25, Reel 115; Drummond to Bradfords, January 7, March 11, 1874, both in M25, Reel 117. Drummond to C. B. Darrall, February 18, March 18, 1874, and Curtis to Darrall, May 29, 1874, all in Division "C," Letters Sent to Members of Congress; R. H. Bradford to Commissioner, March 7, 1874, in MLR, K–91488.

17. GLO to John Tully, June 4, 1867, GLO to R&R, Clarksville, July 7, 1869, both in Letters Sent.

Wilson brought charges against him for nonresidency. Smith claimed that he had not made a permanent home within the requisite six months because of "severe sickness at times, and feeble health generally." During the hearing before the register and receiver, Wilson and Smith admitted that they had worked out a deal whereby Smith would move on the land "to prevent a Negro from going on it," and the property would be divided between the two men. Wilson pleaded ignorance concerning the illegality of the sale or transfer of lands under the Southern Homestead Act, and it could be assumed that he initiated the case to obtain the plot himself.

The local officers split in their opinions. Register D. S. Griffin sided with Smith, alleging he had shown intention to establish his homestead by sowing a few oats, but that sickness had prevented his establishing residency. Receiver A. Tufts disagreed, following a strict construction of the law. Because Smith had not moved upon and resided on the land, because his improvements "were simply an evasion of the law," because he moved on the land only after Wilson contested the entry, and because the law made no provision for "non-compliance . . . on account of sickness or inability," Tufts recommended cancellation. Commissioner Drummond supported Tufts's view. When the case was appealed to Interior Secretary Delano, he upheld the GLO and recommended cancellation because "Smith had no residence on the tract until fourteen months after entry, and his good faith in making such entry is, to say the least, questionable."[18]

It is impossible to delineate every type of conflict that occurred concerning the southern public lands, but one clash could have happened only during this period, namely, the confrontation between the settler who remained loyal to the Union during the war and the rebel. The tensions in the section were common, and it was

18. Papers in case of Joseph G. Wilson versus William E. Smith: Depositions, August 10, 1871, of H. M. Reynolds, Wells H. Wilson, Theodore Wilson, W. E. Smith, William H. Smith, Theodore L. Pedron, and Joseph G. Wilson; Griffin to Commissioner and Tufts to Commissioner, August 14, 1871, W. E. Smith to Drummond, October 2, 1871, C. Delano to Drummond, January 1, 1872, all in MLR, I–79185.

inevitable that they would manifest themselves over claims to public lands.

One Unionist family in the Clarksville district had improvements on land that they had not yet officially applied for when the war came. The head of the household enlisted in the Union army. He died during the war, leaving his widow and five children alone in a hostile area. After the war, the widow tried to manage it on her own, with every intention of acquiring full title to the land. Because times were hard, she made the mistake of accepting an offer of a work horse in exchange for some of her land from "a man [from Texas] who had been in the *rebel* army." After only a week's time, the man returned to the widow, insisted that the land was homesteaded by someone else, and took his horse back. The widow knew his claim was "a falsehood of his own manufacturing," and she sent her homestead papers to Clarksville, but the Texan beat her to the office. The widow hoped that the GLO would understand her plight and not allow the rascal to appropriate for himself the improvements that she and her husband had made.[19]

During the war, John P. Taylor left his native Mississippi to enlist in the 14th Illinois Cavalry. After Appomattox, he returned home and took out a certain plot under the homestead act, only to find it already occupied by a "mr. Mcinis." Taylor minced no words in making his case: "The said mcinis was and is a strong secessionous and in the time of the war Put up President Lincoln Profile and shot at it very often." Not only that, he already owned property; some he had purchased, the rest he had received under the Southern Homestead Act. Taylor wanted orders from Washington to kick the scoundrel off the land. The GLO did not see it his way. The commissioner ordered Taylor's entry canceled, since he had tried to move onto land which had improvements on it.[20]

Whether John Taylor lost confidence in the GLO will never be known, but his case was only one of thousands that came before the

19. J. A. Fair to Wilson, April 5, 1870, in MLR, H–98298.

20. John P. Taylor, April 29, 1867, in MLR, H–4014; GLO to R&R, Jackson, August 13, 1867, in Letters Sent.

office between 1866 and 1876. The manner in which Washington handled these pleas, the ways these cases helped shape federal land policy, and the things they tell us about the actual settlers are all instructive. In short, the true operation of the Southern Homestead Act points up a string of inadequacies, ineptness, and sometimes unreasonable policies that seem out of place under the agrarian vision of the law.

But getting the land is only part of that story. Keeping it is the other. Whereas many never got far past the first stages of homesteading, some who managed to get land had problems meeting the law's requirements. In the end, many of these people were also plucked off their plots. Four major issues dominated the settlers' saga—land quality, violence, difficulties in following the letter of the law, and the trials of proving full compliance.

The poor quality of much of the southern public lands was well known, at least in the South. The variety of evidence available indicates that most of the public land was sandy, swampy, or forested. Other plots that might have been cultivable were off limits because they had not been surveyed; the Southern Homestead Act allowed settlement only on surveyed acreage. In short, only a small portion of available land was cultivable. W. E. Dale too late learned the lesson of entering a claim without first seeing the plot. In the summer of 1869, he applied for a homestead in Putnam County, Florida, "very foolishly, without seeing it. After the certificate issued I visited the land, luckily at a dry time, so I was enabled to see it." As he explained, "It was subject to 'overflow.' "[21]

The second problem in holding on to one's claim issued from the spirit of vindictiveness that prevailed after the Civil War. James M. Small, of Alabama, located a homestead and bought the abandoned improvements already on it, but vandals destroyed his house. He rebuilt, but believed that he still faced dangers. He tried to explain those fears: "If I loose the improve ment a gain and what I have paid and Bee turned out of house and home which with a house full of

21. W. E. Dale to Commissioner, August 23, 1875, in MLR, L–67190.

little children the Reason I am Sopore is Bee cause I have Been Broken up By Disguised clans of KK and the Reason I am Bothered is Bee cause I Report thear conduct to the US. martial." He hoped he could count on assistance, he explained, "as I don as much as I did in the last election."[22]

W. A. McKinney, of Maysville, Arkansas, had his house torn down by former Confederates. He had served four years in the Union army and was "notified" to leave the county "on penalty of death." Why? "No damned Yankee should live on that land." Protesting that there was "no civil law in Benton County Ark. for a poor union man," McKinney wondered how he could demonstrate settlement to gain title, because the only proof he had settled on the land—his house—had been destroyed.[23]

McKinney's dilemma stemmed from his Union service, but other homesteaders also had difficulties unrelated to violence or physical abuse. For countless reasons, many who had tried to comply with the law could not live up to its letter. Some indication of the extent of their failures came from Alabama: the GLO reported in the spring of 1874 that over one-fourth of the fourteen thousand homestead entries made in that state had been suspended.[24]

One reason for failure to comply was a misunderstanding of the requirements. If land officers so often proved ignorant of the rules, it is understandable that homesteaders would also misinterpret or fail to learn of some provision of the law. W. H. Hyde, of Alabama, believed, and the register had so informed him, that either settlement *or* cultivation would fulfill homesteading requirements. Hyde decided to cultivate his entry; he cleared, fenced, and improved ten acres, but never moved onto the tract. He therefore failed to meet the requirements of settlement *and* cultivation.[25]

Many homesteaders found it difficult to settle on the land within

22. James M. Small to Commissioner, November 15, 1872, in MLR, K–23705.
23. W. A. McKinney to Commissioner, December 1, 1869 (letter says 1870), in MLR, H–87338.
24. Curtis to Congressman C. C. Sheats, April 30, 1874, in Division "C," Letters Sent to Members of Congress, RG 49.
25. W. H. Hyde to Drummond, January 29, 1875, in MLR, L–38594.

the requisite six months after filing. Samuel R. Hovey entered a plot in the Montgomery office in August, 1869, but because of "business arrangements" was unable to move on it within the time required by law. By May, 1870, nine months later, he was ready and was allowed to do so. Agents who searched for convenient places for colonists to settle noted that the six-month settlement period was too "short a time to get the parties to the place to commence permanent residence."[26] The dilemmas of these experienced agents revealed that many of the law's requirements were unrealistic.

Too often, land officers refused to budge from unreasonable demands. C. H. Cheatham, for example, had entered eighty acres in the Montgomery district and was in the process of building a comfortable dwelling. He surmounted difficulties in getting lumber for floors and windows and finally finished the house; just before he moved in, the place was "consumed by fire," thereby rendering his compliance impossible. He lost it all.[27]

Robert Wiggins' story was not so tragic, but his personal circumstances prevented him from fulfilling the law's mandates. Wiggins, an itinerant preacher from Florida, entered a homestead in 1868 and began improving it. When he received orders from church superiors to move in January, 1869, he realized that he could not meet the law's residency requirements. He wanted a home and farm for the future, but he was forced to choose between his bishop's orders and the Southern Homestead Act's requirements. He chose his bishop.[28]

James Smith and his wife faced a different set of obstacles. Old age made it impossible for them to perform their duties under the homestead law. Having taken a claim in 1869, the Smiths had cleared the land and fenced and cultivated ten acres. But because he was sixty-nine and she was seventy-two and a "bad Cripple," they found themselves unable to build a house to live in on the land. They

26. Samuel R. Hovey to Wilson, May 7, 1870, in MLR, I–1560; Lewis M. Douglas to Commissioner, July 6, 1872, in MLR, K–5578.

27. C. H. Cheatham to Commissioner, October 26, 1871, in MLR, I–69112.

28. Robert L. Wiggins to Wilson, October 15, 1868, in MLR, H–45226.

must have felt their pleas had fallen on deaf ears when the GLO ruled that they could not obtain a title.[29]

Undoubtedly the greatest frustration came when homesteaders discovered, after several years, much investment, and hard work, that land officers had made errors somewhere along the way. Administrative inadequacies often led to many having their hard-worked claims ripped out from under them. The misery of hundreds can be summed up by H. J. Pile, a barely literate, but quite disturbed, victim of administrative entanglements. Pile had taken out a homestead in Franklin County, Arkansas, probably in early 1868. He found out, after he had made improvements and begun breaking ground for cultivation, that a man somewhere up north "not comeatabil by me" had a patent on the plot. His was not the only case of conflict; as he explained, "Thair is no sertainty in aney of our home steads entered at the Clarkesvill land office [as] thair has bin several hom stid Entries made on pattented land." He knew right where to place the blame: "I want to no if I am to loose money and labor in this way for blunders made by Goverment officiers."[30]

Strict compliance with the law in all of its detail did not necessarily mean that the way was clear for patenting. Final proof of full compliance could still deny final title. Sometimes local officers failed to follow GLO procedures. For example, the officers in Gainesville did not give, as they were required to do, the reasons final affidavits taken before county clerks had not been sworn at the local office. The Jackson officers had a habit of taking testimony from a witness who would swear that a homesteader had lived on his land for five years, but then also swear that he had known the settler for only three years. The commissioner painstakingly explained to his officers, "Witnesses swearing that the homesteader has lived upon the land embraced in his entry a *certain length of time* should be able

29. James M. Smith to Drummond, August 2, 1875, in MLR, L–65842; Curtis to Smith, August 25, 1875, in M25, Reel 121.

30. H. J. Pile to Commissioner, April 7, 1868, in MLR, H–31063; Pile to Wilson, February 19, 1868, in MLR, H–56402.

to make oath that they have known the party for at least an equal period."[31]

Frequently, settlers who had cultivated a plot for as many as seven years discovered that they could not get clear title. In many of these cases, the homesteader had originally entered double the land he was entitled to under the law. Almost without exception, the error was discovered only at the time of final patenting. Jonathan C. Gibbs, secretary of state of Florida, conveyed his irritation when he discovered that forty of the eighty acres he had been cultivating and settling were not his. As he explained, "Now as the time approaches for procuring a patent, I am informed that 40 acres is all that I can get a Patent for."[32]

The General Land Office was not without compassion, but it moved slowly to change fundamental procedures. After it was so deluged with the acreage reduction problem, the GLO modified its policy. In a statement to the land officers in Little Rock, the commissioner, empathizing with the settlers' perplexities, allowed final proof to be made. He wrote, "I have to state that it would seem at this late day, manifestly unjust, to restrict them to 40 acres which doubtless in many cases would work serious damage to the homestead parties." If proof showed bona fide settlement and cultivation, he would submit the cases for confirmation of full acreage to a board of adjudication.[33]

Whether because of compassion or force of appeal, the GLO revised its policy. It was not always so generous, though, as Samuel C. Gerrald, of Arkansas, would be quick to point out. When Gerrald found no water on his plot, he built his house and began cultivation "within twenty steps" of his claim. In 1875, the GLO disallowed his final proof because "under no circumstances can residence on a homestead entry be dispensed with."[34] Gerrald must have felt that

31. GLO to R&R, Gainesville, September 21, 1875, GLO to R&R, Jackson, December 2, 1875, both in Letters Sent (emphasis in original).

32. Jonathan C. Gibbs to Drummond, November 21, 1871, in MLR, I–72315.

33. GLO to R&R, Little Rock, September 16, 1872, in Letters Sent.

34. GLO to R&R, Camden, August 21, 1875, in Letters Sent.

the General Land Office was picking on him when it disallowed his entry for a mere twenty steps. But there were many cases of a similar nature.

Some homesteaders simply found it impossible to get to a land office to obtain their deeds. True, an 1864 revision of the original Homestead Act allowed final proof to be made before the clerk of the court of the county of residence if the settler was "prevented, by reason of distance, bodily infirmity, or other good cause, from personal attendance at the district land-office." But some homesteaders were too poor, old, put-upon, and handicapped to reach the proper authorities to validate their deeds. Jairus Norton was blind and poor; John Ferguson was "old and infirm" and lived eighty miles from the local office. Philip Hefner was seventy-eight years old, "very feeble and unable to take care of himself." Receiver S. F. Halliday told more about land quality than distance to the local office when he summed up the situation for some of the settlers in the Gainesville district: "If they should be required to go in person before the Officers of the Land Office with their witnesses in this Land District, it will cost them in many instances more than their lands are worth."[35]

George C. McKee, congressman from Mississippi, recounted the problems and feelings of those in his state, which had only one land office where settlers could conduct business, when he said:

It can hardly be understood in Washington how poor these fellows are. They have been scratching along with poor crop years, low prices, high taxes and far from market. We have but one Land Office in the State. Many probably most of these parties must travel from 200 to 400 miles going and returning. It will cost them from $30 to $50 to make the trip. *They have not got the money.* It is not the cost of the $2 or $4 fees that bothers them; it is the time trouble and expense of getting a chance to pay out this petty sum. And because of their inability to come to Jackson, these entries are rapidly drifting back on the books, to the damage and annoyance of the U.S.—of the

35. GLO to R&R, Huntsville, May 21, 1875, in Letters Sent; John M. Ferguson to Commissioner, June 16, 1873, in MLR, K–55934; S. F. Halliday to Commissioner, February 2, 1872, in MLR, I–80689; GLO to R&R, Huntsville, July 14, 1874, in Letters Sent.

State—and especially of the homesteader, for whose special benefit the law was made. *Several thousand* of the poor fellows are now on the point of losing their incompleted homestead. They all plead poverty and distance.[36]

Some homesteaders fulfilled all their obligations but did not make final proof in the time allowed—from five to seven years after applying. There was always a reason. John Skeen, of Florida, was "totally disabled by the loss of his eyesight." Jefferson Brooks, also of Florida, did not know about the time constraints. Amy Harris, living in Alabama, was old and crippled. In most of these cases, the GLO showed some sympathy. Because the cancellation of a claim would work such hardships, the GLO ruled that settlers could have their papers submitted to the Board of Adjudication for a final decision.[37]

These setbacks during final proof were only the last obstacles in the long journey to securing homes on the federal lands. Policies of the GLO too often seemed to stymie rather than fulfill the goals of the original law. The homestead principle assumed a vision of individual landownership, and the law detailed a simple process for turning that vision into a reality. Getting and keeping the land, however, proved not to be as simple as the benevolent homestead principle promised. The actual settlers knew more about the implications of the law than the framers did. Often poor, sometimes elderly, but always hopeful, homesteaders desperately tried to obtain land of their own. Among these were the thousands of freedmen who would have similar problems—but some unique ones, too—in searching for lands of their own.

36. George C. McKee to Burdett, April 28, 1875, in MLR, L–50336.

37. GLO to R&R, Gainesville, March 8, 1876, June 2, 1875, GLO to R&R, Montgomery, March 5, 1875, GLO to R&R, Jackson, July 10, 1875, all in Letters Sent.

IV

"We Are Now Readeay To Go Theare"

The sponsors of the Southern Homestead Act understood the critical importance of providing land to the impecunious former slaves because, they reasoned, freedom would be meaningless without an economic basis. Most other Republican leaders, however, in granting black southerners political and legal rights, felt their duty was fulfilled; they did not earnestly try to provide freedmen any social or economic rights.

Accomplishing such additional objectives would have required a massive reorganization in southern land tenure, but it was seldom suggested and little action was ever taken on the matter. The Southern Homestead Act represented a moderate effort to solve the problem of providing land. Because it flowed from existing legislation, it did not greatly disturb the Republican majority in Congress. True, southerners feared that black landownership would cause a severe labor shortage and thus actively opposed freedmen leaving the plantations to become landowners, but their resistance was not the only reason that the promise of land under the Southern Homestead Act proved elusive. Republican leaders failed to pursue the bill's original policies of helping the freedmen. The law, moreover, had little meaning for people who began with nothing and had no capital to start a farm—even with free land. The assurance of homestead land for the freedmen proved, in the end, to be nothing more than another dream deferred.

The desire for land among the freedmen was remarkably strong.

They considered land as both a symbol of freedom and a real means of making a living. Black people tried to retain land they had worked before and during the Civil War. Their conventions regularly called for land along with education and the suffrage. Some resisted contracting out their labor, preferring to remain independent farmers rather than becoming sharecroppers. Their eagerness and willingness to obtain property and make it productive, coupled with their magnified expectations of receiving it, account for the fervent and passionate attempts to turn promises into reality. The organization of all-black communities, the success of experiments in self-government, such as in Davis Bend, Mississippi, and the many examples of organized bodies of freedmen moving to certain sites, such as New Smyrna, Florida, all demonstrate the lure of the land. Those who have studied the connection between the freedmen and the land have found an important and significant bond between the acquisition of land and the formation of the freedmen's community. The freedmen shared with other Americans the values of self-help, self-support, and hard work. Their pursuit of the nineteenth-century American dream—an independent homestead—reflected their desires to live the life that most Americans lived.[1]

The passage of the Southern Homestead Act dramatically whetted the appetites of many former slaves. Black people, aware that the law had been passed, joined thousands of other prospective homesteaders in trying to find out more about it. Many wrote directly to the General Land Office in Washington. Their notes indicated a willingness to work and to earn a living free of restraints. Perhaps most important, they shared with other Americans the nineteenth-century belief that landownership would solve all problems and help to reform society. But once it materialized, the vision of landownership was even more deeply felt by black Americans, long denied access to the largess of the continent.

1. Edward Magdol, *A Right to the Land: Essays on the Freedmen's Community* (Westport, Conn., 1977), *passim*, but especially pp. 17 and 73; Oscar Zeichner, "The Transition from Slave to Free Agricultural Labor in the Southern States," *Agricultural History*, XIII (1939), 23; Janet Sharp Hermann, *The Pursuit of a Dream* (New York, 1981).

The note of John Churchill and Henry Cole, both of Washington County, Florida, in August, 1866, is typical. They first stated that they had "bin freed by president Lincon s procolamation," then went on: "We are willing to pay the government price and if we can get writings to put us in possession as the white people try to oppress us in every way possible [.] We are all willing to work and if we can only have a fair chance we can easily pay for our lands [. I]f you can do anything please let [us] know with out delay."[2]

Like Churchill and Cole, Harmey Smith, of the same county, in obvious reference to the Southern Homestead Act, sounded a variation on the theme of forty acres and a mule: "Having bin given to understand that all colored people that has bin freed can have eighty acers of land where ever there is any public land if that is the case I wish to draw my land in this state and county."[3]

Freedmen deluged local land officers with requests for land shortly after the passage of the act. Register William Carruth, of Washington, Arkansas, reported in September that the freedmen were "anxious (many of them) to purchase a homestead for actual settlement, and applications from them are hourly made at this office." The same month, the U.S. attorney in southern Mississippi reported that freedmen were daily asking him about public land in southeastern Mississippi. Henry Myers reported from Natchitoches in July, 1867, that his hands were tied because "large number[s] of colored people are daily endeavoring to procure homes" in the Fort Jesup reservation. Because it was reserved for military purposes, he was unable to act on their requests.[4] Whether the officers' reports were exaggerated is not important; what is clear is that freedmen joined the appeals for land.

Among these countless inquiries and requests, none was more touching in its style and simplicity than the one from Owen Jones, a former slave from New Bern, North Carolina. His note was written

2. John Churchill and Henry Cole to GLO, August 30, 1866, in MLR, G–86889.

3. Harmey Smith to GLO, August 31, 1866, in MLR, G–86939.

4. William Carruth to Edmunds, September 8, 1866, in MLR, G–87152; R. Leachman to O. Browning (forwarded to GLO), September 18, 1866, in MLR, G–87396; Henry C. Myers to Joseph Wilson, July 16, 1867, in MLR, H–10207.

on half a sheet of scrap paper and is barely legible, but his message rings out clearly. Its closing words spoke powerfully of the collective hopes of the freedmen: "As your Dear Obedeant Searvant Sir Asketh off you A favear Sir will you Please to grant that to me: Sir will you Sir soon devise [?] A way for 40 men to go down to florideay on that land that the government Has orfered the Coleared people Sir we are Now Readeay to go theare."[5]

Yet the freedmen would be sorely disappointed. The obstacles that blocked the way of the white homesteaders were to prove at least as troublesome to their black counterparts. Getting the land and keeping it were color-blind difficulties, but the former slaves had their own unique problems.

Some congressmen realized the obstacles that freedmen faced under the Southern Homestead Act, and they attempted to aid them in securing title to the public lands, even though they failed to get any additional legislation. A resolution introduced by Charles Sumner in July, 1867, required all rebel landowners, before they received pardons, to convey part of their land to their former slaves "so that they may have a homestead in which their own labor has mingled." A few days later, Representative Halbert Paine of Wisconsin introduced a bill authorizing the Freedmen's Bureau to employ a surveyor in each southern land district to clarify disputed property boundaries. The bill would also have required the commissioner of the GLO to furnish to the Freedmen's Bureau whatever information was necessary to help freedmen locate homesteads. Paine's legislation died in committee. The indefatigable George Julian ceaselessly tried to secure legislation in behalf of the freedmen. In early 1870, he introduced a resolution calling for the appointment of a land commissioner whose sole duty was to help freedmen and other landless people in the South acquire homesteads. Nothing more was ever done.[6]

5. Owen Jones to GLO, January 18, 1868, in MLR, H–22816.

6. *Congressional Globe,* 40th Cong., 1st Sess., 467; H.R. 122, *A Bill to Facilitate the Occupation of Public Lands by Freedmen Under the Homestead Act,* 40th Cong., 1st Sess., 1867; *Congressional Globe,* 41st Cong., 2nd Sess., 794.

Representative Samuel Arnell of Tennessee sponsored, on February 6, 1871, the most important piece of federal legislation designed not only to help freedmen obtain property but also to protect them in their rights to the land—a bill to incorporate the Freedmen's Homestead Company. The legislation, which never made it past the Committee on Reconstruction, named several prominent figures as the company's trustees—Frederick Douglass, O. O. Howard, John M. Langston, James T. Rapier, and Oscar Dunn, among others. The purpose of this corporation was "to aid in procuring homesteads" in the southern states and "to assist in the settlement thereon of persons formerly held in slavery and their descendants, and to foster industrial pursuits, co-operative enterprises, and the acquirement of useful knowledge among them." Its headquarters were to be in Washington, with branches and agencies elsewhere, and its affairs were to be under the watchful eye of Congress.

The sixth section of the bill was the most significant, because it set forth punishments for those trying to deny freedmen their rights under the homestead laws. Specifically, it stated that any person who interfered in any way with an officer or agent of the corporation, or who intimidated, prevented, or obstructed any freedmen from occupying a homestead would be guilty of a criminal offense, punishable by fine and imprisonment. The federal courts had exclusive jurisdiction. The bill further stated that if proceedings against the corporation or its beneficiaries were brought in state court, the defendant could move the trial to federal court under either the Habeas Corpus Act of 1863 or the Civil Rights Act of 1866.[7] Clearly, Arnell and other Republicans believed that the federal government had a responsibility to help former slaves secure federal lands and, beyond that, to protect them in their legal rights.

If Congress took no successful steps to help the freedmen, the Freedmen's Bureau did. Despite some insincere efforts on the part of some agents, Commissioner Oliver O. Howard and his subordi-

7. H.R. 2970, *A Bill to Incorporate the Freedmen's Homestead Company,* 41st Cong., 3rd Sess., 1871.

nates made some valiant attempts to help freedmen acquire homesteads. Howard issued his Circular 7 less than two weeks after Andrew Johnson signed the Southern Homestead Act in June, 1866. After setting forth the legislation, Howard instructed the assistant commissioners to move quickly, because the remaining six months of the year provided unparalleled opportunities for freedmen to obtain homes. He obviously believed that this piece of legislation was the realization of a government promise, because he commented that settlement on public lands would likely "secure" homesteaders "from any interference likely to occur." Perhaps he was referring to Johnson's pardoning policy, which resulted in the return of confiscated lands to their former owners.

Before giving the locations of the land offices, Howard made one last request for positive action: "Information of the location and quality of lands, the manner of entry, the advantage of this offer of the Government, the increased security, and many reasons for companies of these people entering lands lying contiguous, should be collected and presented in the strongest manner." Several southern newspapers published the circular in its entirety; others reported that it had been issued.[8]

Some state agents of the bureau tried to execute Howard's instructions almost immediately. In Louisiana, Assistant Commissioner Absalom Baird appointed J. J. Saville as locating agent on July 15. Baird ordered Saville to give information and execute legal documents for loyal refugees and freedmen. He also urged quick action to take advantage of the act's temporary prohibitions on former Confederates and even said that the Freedmen's Bureau would pay homestead fees if Howard approved. By January, 1867, Saville, ever eager to execute his duties and untiring in his efforts, had settled eighty-seven freedmen on public lands and expressed dissatisfaction over injustices perpetrated against the former slaves. He also tried to secure the lands of the New Orleans, Opelousas, and Great Western Railroad for homesteads, but con-

8. O. O. Howard, Circular 7, July 2, 1866, quoted in the Huntsville *Advocate*, July 11, 1866.

gressional inaction delayed these efforts. In July, 1867, Saville reported that about one hundred families intended to homestead by September, with several hundred more to follow in the fall and winter.[9]

Nothing went smoothly for Saville. The New Orleans land office was closed throughout most of his appointment, and very few freedmen actually filed official papers. In addition, John Tully, register in New Orleans, complained that Saville was interfering with the register's official duties, deluding the freedmen by charging them "exorbitant" fees, and locating them on land not belonging to the government. Several freedmen, he claimed, had complained about Saville's irregular actions.

There is evidence to support the contention that Saville was charging incorrect fees, but this can be blamed on ignorance of the law—surely a trait Saville shared with other land officers. However, his general actions are praiseworthy, considering his efforts to help the freedmen, the tangled nature of the land office business, and his attempts to alert Congress to some of the realities of public land needs in Louisiana, such as railroad forfeits.[10]

Bureau agents like Saville took Howard's orders to heart and did their best to help settle freedmen. They conducted surveys, requested pertinent information such as township plats and other records, and provided other needed services. When the supply of "abandoned lands" began to dwindle, the bureau turned to federal lands to take up the slack.[11]

Locating agents working in the South were less organized and often without official standing, but they did their part in helping the freedmen. Their assistance was necessary, and freedmen relied on them to overcome some of the hardships accompanying public land

9. New Orleans *Times*, July 27, 1866. For an account of Saville's efforts and setbacks, see Oubre, *Forty Acres*, 117–30.

10. John Tully to Wilson, October 31, 1866, in MLR, G–89540. See also Oubre, *Forty Acres*, 120.

11. For a full account of the Freedmen's Bureau and its efforts to secure land for the freedmen, see Oubre, *Forty Acres*.

acquisition. They performed valuable jobs in helping to establish boundaries, determine plots, and file the required papers.

David S. White, of Marion County, Florida, wanted township maps because the freedmen "are ever & again applying to me to select & locate for them a tract of land." C. W. Gallagher, of Paulding, Mississippi, wanted a commission so he could locate freedmen on lands in his vicinity, for they "are anxious to locate it under the law." Jonathan Cory, of Jacksonville, a Presbyterian teacher in the freedmen schools who had tried to find homes for refugees and freedmen, found that this activity took a great deal of time. The services of locating agents allowed him to return to teaching.[12]

When it came to getting the land, one significant difference existed between whites and blacks: whites usually located individually, but blacks often moved in colonies to the public lands. Letters from both private parties and agents of the Freedmen's Bureau frequently spoke of "colonies" of freedmen. The settlement in New Smyrna, Florida, was only the most prominent example. James Fitz Allan Sisson, an African Methodist Episcopal pastor in Decatur, Georgia, along with members of his congregation, wanted to homestead in Florida. W. H. F. Hall, a former member of the Georgia Legislature, asked about the possibility of several black families homesteading in Arkansas. Edward Magdol sees these organizations of freedmen, actively and collectively seeking a change of location, as a cooperative movement, helping to build and reinforce what he calls "habits of mutuality."[13]

Once a black person obtained public land, he had to try to keep it, and keeping the land proved more difficult for the freedmen than for the whites. True, both groups encountered similar problems, like conflicting claims, corruption and ineptness of local officers, and

12. David S. White to Commissioner, October 26, 1866, in MLR, G–89590; C. W. Gallagher to Messrs. Henry and Walker (forwarded to GLO), November 29, 1866, in MLR, G–91354; Jonathan Cory to Wilson, March 28, 1867, in MLR, H–258.

13. Oubre, *Forty Acres*, 144–147; James Fitz Allan Sisson to Commissioner, May 17, 1870, in MLR, I–3665; W. H. F. Hall to Commissioner, April 18, 1873, in MLR, K–45958; Magdol, *Right to the Land*, 189, and *passim*.

cancellations, but black claimants also faced prejudice and racial discrimination.

Like their white counterparts, black homesteaders sometimes found their small holdings located on reserved land. John Thomas, Jackson Brown, and George and John Irvin, all freedmen, settled on land also claimed by the Little Rock and Fort Smith Railroad. This particular case was complicated by the fact that the exact status of the railroad land was unclear when the four men made their entries. Eventually, the GLO canceled their claims.[14]

Charlotte Henry, a "teacher of freedmen," was more successful. She entered about 150 homesteads for freedmen near Palatka, Florida, in July, 1867. Register Stonelake gave her the necessary papers, but it was later discovered that the lands she claimed were state, not federal, lands. Commissioner Wilson finally resolved the dilemma. The federal government had reserved that particular area for military purposes in 1841, but restored it to market in 1858. The state had indeed selected some of that land for swamp reclamation, but had done so while the land was still a military reservation. The GLO, therefore, rejected the state's claim, thereby ruling the lands public, and the homestead entries would not be disturbed.[15]

The General Land Office kept no records of race in its operations and never made official recognition of color. But its policy was not evenhanded. GLO officials openly tolerated prejudicial treatment of freedmen by their local officers, in violation of the Southern Homestead Act's specific provision against discrimination. The corruption and ineptness of local officers touched both blacks and whites, but at times the officers knew the color of the homesteaders and acted against their interests.

14. J. H. Haney to Wilson, December 9, 1867, in MLR, H–19794; W. W. Granger to George W. Denison, May 19, 1868, in MLR, H–33686. The parties appealed to the secretary of the interior, but his decision is unknown because the letter with his reply cannot be found.

15. Charlotte Henry to Schuyler Colfax, December 16, 1867, in Register of MLR, H–20382; Henry to Wilson, January 8, 1868, in MLR, H–21998; Commissioner to Henry, January 20, 1868, in M25, Reel 99, Register of Miscellaneous Letters Sent, RG 49.

One problem that the freedmen found especially troublesome was the charging of illegal fees. The less-than-honest register of Mobile, Salmon Dutton, charged higher fees, particularly to black homesteaders. James Gillette, sub-assistant commissioner of the Freedmen's Bureau in Mobile, tried to bring this irregularity to Dutton's attention. Dutton's practically illegible reply was brief and curt. He declined to answer the allegations about his fees and arrogantly retorted, "That is optional with me if a *man* can enter at all. . . . If he does so it is because I allow him not that I am in duty bound." Some freedmen paid between twenty-five and forty dollars for the land alone, plus an additional twenty dollars to have it surveyed. Gillette maintained, "The intention of the Homestead Act is practically defeated." It is evident that many freedmen were caught in Dutton's trap, judging by the complaints they filed with Gillette, who sent them on to O. O. Howard.[16]

If higher fees could not keep blacks off the land, there were other barriers. M. P. Johnson, a white man, entered two tracts of land totaling 164 acres and paid the register $1.25 an acre. Cash payments were, of course, illegal under the Southern Homestead Act. Why did Dutton allow it? Johnson explained: the very same land "had been taken up as homesteads by negroes & . . . they had paid Duttons fees on it, but as I did not want them to settle so near to me . . . I could displace them by paying him for the land."[17] Johnson did not want a "mixed" neighborhood and Dutton gladly satisfied his wish.

Only three and a half months after the Southern Homestead Act became law, Tallahassee Register A. B. Stonelake craftily pleaded to the GLO the case of a white woman against a poor freedman. He began with an honest observation of how the six-month exclusion-

16. James Gillette to Salmon Dutton, May 12, 1868, Dutton to Gillette, May 13, 1868, both in Appointments, Alabama; Gillette to Assistant Commissioner, May 29, 1868 (endorsed by Howard to the GLO Commissioner with several affidavits), in MLR, H–34805.

17. Statement of James Tharp (recounting M. P. Johnson's story), August 13, 1868, in Appointments, Alabama.

ary period worked. Stonelake reported that because many of the area residents were former Confederates and did not qualify for land in October of 1866, freedmen were entering the land "and cases of positive distress are occuring in consequence"—distress undoubtedly among the white people. The freedman in this case had come to the land office in Tallahassee to enter a certain tract. The land he wanted already had a house on it occupied by a Confederate soldier's widow. Stonelake issued to the freedman, Nat Goodman, a receipt that indicated Goodman had paid his fees. Fifteen minutes after the black man left the office, someone came in and informed Stonelake that a Dr. Mitchell wanted to gain possession of land "through the instrumentality of eight of his former slaves." One of them was Goodman. Suddenly and without explanation, Stonelake decided that the widow occupying the land could take the oath and qualify to take advantage of the homestead act. At about the same time, he also discovered some error in the description of the land he had given to Goodman. He therefore believed it was his duty "to recover that receipt" from the freedman, and he did. After carefully weighing all the evidence, the register and receiver decided to give the widow a receipt, because she deserved one. Stonelake assured the commissioner at the end of his tale, "I have no prejudices and desire to fulfil my duties conscientiously." He asked if he had done the right thing.[18]

The commissioner reaffirmed the government's policy. All sales of public lands by the Confederate states during the war were null and void, but the GLO was willing to grant preference rights to those already settled on them. Commissioner Wilson reiterated what was to become repetitive: "It is not the policy or practice of the Department to allow one man to appropriate the fruits of anothers labor without consideration."[19] This meant the Confederate widow would get the land.

J. F. H. Claiborne, U.S. commissioner in southern Mississippi, in

18. Stonelake to Wilson, October 5, 1866, in MLR, G–88449.

19. Wilson to R&R, Tallahassee, October 20, 1866, in Letters Sent. It will be remembered that that policy was changing by the 1870s.

early 1867 tried to assist people living along the Gulf coast. Many were poor whites, "mostly refugees from the interior of the state," who lived "on the food furnished by our salt water coasts and inlets." The rest were the freedmen. Claiborne helped about 120 of these people to fill out applications and meet other requirements. He was shocked to discover that he, as U.S. commissioner, could not administer the oath, that only a county clerk could do so. He painted a dismal portrait of these hopeful people:

> The fact is, the majority of the applicants never would have procured the clerks certificate; many of them could not pay his fee; many are women; some sick; some aged and crippled; few have horses or conveyances; and some would not, under any circumstances, appear before [the clerk], he having been a Captain in the Confed. armies, charged with the duty of conscription & had in the remorseless exercise of his functions, driven from their homes many of these very applicants. Nor could they be made to understand how it was, that they must appear before *him,* instead of the *Commissioner* specially charged, in his instructions, to give these two classes of people every protection in his power.

Claiborne simply could not understand how the simple swearing of an affidavit before a U.S. commissioner instead of a county clerk could keep a potential 1,000 applicants, "chiefly freedmen," from settling on the Mississippi coast.[20]

Stonelake confirmed these realities. He discovered that Tallahassee was doing less than half the business anticipated because applicants were making their affidavits before the wrong officers. The vast majority of future homesteaders were illiterate, and Stonelake found it almost impossible to contact them. The register warned that if "this informality [concerning affidavits]" deprived them of their land, these unfortunate circumstances would surely confirm a rumor already circulating among them: "The government at some future time intends to deprive them (I speak more especially of the Freedmen) of the lands they are now entering."[21]

A group of black homesteaders in Arkansas pointed to another

20. J. F. H. Claiborne to Wilson, January 13, 1867, in MLR, G–94429.
21. Stonelake to Wilson, January 31, 1867, in MLR, G–96681.

problem, namely, the impracticality of living on their tracts for five years, especially when they had to try to support themselves at the same time. Five black men took homesteads in Arkansas in the fall of 1871, and within six months, as the law required, moved onto them and built their houses. But spring came, and they found themselves unable, "from lack of financial ability," to clear their lands in order to plant crops that season. Therefore, they rented some land several miles away where they made their crops. Was this abandonment of a homestead and, consequently, grounds for cancellation? The outcome is not known, but GLO settlement requirements caused hardships when homesteaders needed to move in order to work.[22]

Some individuals, mostly land speculators, took advantage of the freedmen's new position, using them to secure land illegally and dumping them once their usefulness had passed. J. H. Sanborn, of Florida, implied that speculators were using black people to perpetrate frauds against the government. He directed the following question to the secretary of the interior: "Can I, or any other person, take 80 or 160 acres of U.S. land as homestead, put a negro man on it for the term of 5 years allowing him all his crops as pay for clearing it up and I meanwhile be doing business in town here, or in New York or Boston—then at end of 5 yrs I demand my papers or patent from the U.S. as if I had done all the work. I then sell the land that has not cost me $10 for the sum of $3000. or more?"[23] The answer was obviously no, but Sanborn's inquiry suggests that such malfeasance was taking place.

Similar improprieties occurred in Mississippi. White people, taking advantage of some freedmen's ignorance of the law, entered hundreds of acres of land under the guise of aiding blacks to get their own land. Because there was usually some violation of the terms of the law, the black man was subject "to punishment and shame." One person complained to the commissioner that whites

22. W. A. Bevens to Commissioner, May 7, 1872, in MLR, I–96952.
23. J. H. Sanborn to Secretary of the Interior, May 7, 1869, in MLR, H–63203.

committed these illegal deeds because "they hate the negro, & hate Republicanism & in a word care not what they do."[24]

Conflicts and cancellations were problems that plagued all homesteaders. Blacks suffered because of inaccurate records, poor surveys, double claims, and all the other anomalies that many southern homesteaders faced. What is most striking, though, is their persistence in homesteading. Despite policy rulings, fear of losing many years of improvements, frustrations, and all the rest, the hardy men and women clung to what they had and made every effort to save their land. The case of a nameless freedman in Alabama could symbolize many more. He had been cultivating a portion of public land for three or four years and had every intention of filing an application. He had even given his money to "a certain official" who was to make the application for him. In the meantime, as in so many cases, someone else made it to the land office first, about May, 1869, and formally filed the papers to claim the same tract. One year later, this person still had not taken possession or even asked the freedman to leave. The freedman hoped the GLO would rule that this was a case of abandonment; then the land would revert to the government and the freedman could make his claim secure.[25]

A case in Arkansas demonstrates how "industrious colored men" were frustrated by inaccurate records. William L. Taylor, an attorney and a locating agent in Crawford County, applied for lands at the Dardanelle office on behalf of some of his clients. The local officers informed him that the lands he had requested were swamplands owned by the state. So he went to Little Rock to apply at the state land office. There he was told that the lands were federal lands. In requesting assistance from the GLO to straighten out the records, Taylor noted that the settlers were black men "who wish to comply with the law" and receive their titles.[26]

24. W. H. B. Lane to Commissioner, October 6, 1870, in MLR, I–20081.
25. E. G. Brewton to Commissioner, May 28, 1870, in MLR, I–3.
26. William L. Taylor to Commissioner, April 9, 1873, in MLR, K–44614.

Julia Yellida, from Yazoo County, Mississippi, was the mother of Robert Yellida, 49th U.S. Colored Troops, who had died at Milliken's Bend. She was determined to have land of her own. Her persistence and her ultimate decision show an unflagging will and a strength that seemed common among the freedmen. Ten years after her son's death, Mrs. Yellida paid an agent twenty-five dollars to locate a homestead for her. He promised to have it in four months. One year later, she was still without her land, but she did not give up. Near the end of Mrs. Yellida's ordeal, the register in Jackson informed her that there was no public land in Yazoo County anyway. That did not stop Julia Yellida. She said she did not care where the plot was, as long as it was not subject to overflow![27] It is not known whether she got land outside Yazoo County, but her determination demonstrated her eagerness to have some.

By the end of 1875, bullying of blacks in Florida and elsewhere had become common. This intimidation, although not confined strictly to politics, extended to homestead claimants as well, especially to those who were about to receive title to their own lands. Many whites feared that landownership conveyed a certain power. In November of that year, J. H. White informed Interior Secretary Zachariah Chandler what was transpiring in Florida. White's sister-in-law went to Florida during the Lincoln administration to teach and care for the freedmen. She could "give a pretty liveley history of the conduct, purposes, and [illegible] of the Florida negro haters, *Democrats*." She had helped many freedmen get homesteads, and it was time for them to prove up their claims and receive their titles. But the "Southern gentry are trying to prevent proper titles getting in the hands of Negroes with an ultimate view of grabing the lands held by the Negroes, when their *starr* is in the assendincy." Mr. White hoped the secretary would aid his sister-in-law, because the secretary was "one of the men who believe in meeting out justice to Negroes and the Rebl. element of the South."[28]

27. John Coleman to "Mr. 2nd Auditor," December 29, 1873, in MLR, K–83611; Coleman to Drummond, February 18, 1874, in MLR, K–90856.

28. J. H. White to Z. Chandler, November 4, 1875, in MLR, L–77133.

Race, then, was a factor in proving up a final claim. Complex southern homestead policy, coupled with discrimination, hindered easy settlement by the freedmen. Each step presented sometimes insurmountable difficulties that were especially acute for poor, illiterate people—black or white. The freedmen's badge of color and previous servitude complicated matters to almost incomprehensible proportions.

Several people on the scene were aware of the obstacles, but they felt as though their hands were tied in trying to help. Jonathan Cory, for example, believed that the local officers in Tallahassee were partly to blame, but there were other problems. He wrote to U. S. Grant in 1867: "Excuse me if I think that the Homestead Act is as much in fault as the officers who execute it. How can the immigrants swear that they reside in a certain State and County when they have no home any where[?] How can they afford to go to the U.S. land office to procure an entry without money enough to sustain their lives a single week at any public boarding house?" Underscoring the intentions of white southerners, he continued, "Many honestly think that the law was made to swindle the poor negro out of his money, and leave him homeless and landless, so as to make labor cheaper in the States in which the U.S. lands lie." Then, in a telling question: "How easy it would be to remove all these difficulties, if Congress and the U.S. land Officers desired to place the poor Whites and Freedmen upon the U.S. lands?"[29]

Cory understood that the homestead act provided nothing to those who had nothing. In fact, this much-heralded legislation was fast becoming much maligned. There were significant obstacles, but black people persisted in trying to acquire land. It is virtually impossible to determine, at least from land office records, exactly how many applied or completed their entries; the land office did not

29. Jonathan Cory to U. S. Grant (copy of letter sent to Wilson), May 11, 1867, in MLR, H–4758. W. W. Granger expressed similar concerns about intentions and problems for the poor. See W. W. Granger to John Kirkwood, Receiver at Little Rock, February 24, 1867, in Registers and Letters Received by the Bureau of Refugees, Freedmen, and Abandoned Lands, 1865–1872, microfilm edition, M752, Reel 42, RG 105.

keep records by race. In view of the stated goals of those who drafted the Southern Homestead Act to help freedmen get land, the policy makers had no way of determining whether or not it actually worked.

However, using a variety of sources, such as the application papers, patent records, and the U.S. census, we can obtain some information about the homesteaders and their lands. Mississippi provides the best starting point because the state had only one land office, in Jackson, during the entire period. That is to say, all homesteaders from throughout the state eventually had to use this office.[30]

Mississippi homesteaders applied for 8,797 plots totaling 758,461 acres while the Southern Homestead Act was in force. This would make the average homestead 86.2 acres. Of the 8,797 applicants, 6,415 failed to acquire title. A race breakdown of the 8,797 applicants is not available. However, estimates based on research samples can be developed. Appendix A notes the severe caveats on the validity of these calculations. However, while we remain conscious of valid criticism, it is useful to view the estimates to see what they might suggest.

The major difficulty in forming estimates is the problem of lost data. Let us assume that missing values are consistent with known values; these results are known as straightforward estimates. Of the 8,797 applicants, 2,008 (22.83 percent) are judged to be black, and 6,789 (77.17 percent) are estimated to be white. (See Appendix A, Table 10.) Table 2 provides the calculations of race representation, broken down by successful and unsuccessful applications.

What is most striking here is that black homesteaders, certainly far fewer in number than whites, were more successful than whites in patenting their homesteads (35 percent to 25 percent). If we accept these estimates as correct, several points can help explain them. Because of their work on plantations, most blacks knew how

30. Appendix A provides a step-by-step analysis of my method of sampling, an important word of caution in using and making conclusions from incomplete data, and the tables from which the composite figures are derived.

TABLE 2
Estimated Totals of Unsuccessful
and Successful Applicants

Race	*Frequency*		*Total*
	Cancelled	Patented	
Black	1,311 (65.29%)	697 (34.71%)	2,008 (100%)
White	5,104 (75.18%)	1,685 (24.82%)	6,789 (100%)
	6,415	2,382	8,797

SOURCE: Appendix A, Tables 8, 9, 10.

to make land productive and to farm. Also, black people were beginning with nothing and striving toward some semblance of freedom. Although no group was very successful at homesteading, black people proved more resourceful in overcoming odds in beginning a new life.

An alternative explanation is that the sample figures are so incomplete that the assessments are spuriously skewed in favor of blacks. A closer look at the data will help evaluate this criticism of the estimates. One can set plausible limits for the extremes that calculations can attain. For example, all the unknown successful applicants could be black and all the unknown unsuccessful applicants, white (best case). Or the reverse could apply: all the unknown successful applicants could be white and the unsuccessful, black (worst case). Or perhaps, all the unknowns, successful and unsuccessful, could be white. This last scenario would produce the smallest percentage of black applicants. Table 3 provides a summary of these best- and worst-case scenarios, along with the straightforward estimates.

Ultimately, what are the best estimates? The best-case estimates of percentage of black applicants (22.63) are almost exactly the same as the straightforward ones (22.83). But the success rate of

TABLE 3
Various Scenarios for Black Representation Among Homesteaders

Estimation Method	*Estimated Black Percent of All Applicants*	*Implied Success Rate*
Best Case	22.63	65.54
Worst Case	47.60	10.65
Smallest Possible Percentage	12.73	39.82
Straightforward	22.83	35.15

SOURCE: Table 2, and Appendix A, pp. 133–34.

almost 66 percent for the best case is a warning of the extremity (and absurdity) of the case. The worst-case calculations make the percentage of black applicants too high, especially in light of the documentary evidence, even though black people made up about 50 percent of Mississippi's population. Again, it is the very low success rate that raises the red flag. It seems safe to say, if we work within these boundaries, that blacks constituted between 20 percent and 25 percent of all applicants and that their success rate was equal to or greater than that of whites.

A closer look at the data for some exceptional counties is illuminating.[31] Carroll and Covington counties had an equal number of canceled and patented applications. Simpson County had the most applicants, forty-five, followed by Hancock County, which had forty-two. Some counties—all the counties along the Mississippi River—had no entries. Much of this rich land was already in private hands by the time of the Civil War. Holmes County had the fewest homesteads—one. The homesteader was black, and he successfully patented his claim. On the other extreme, all the homesteaders in the sample in Copiah, Wilkinson, and Yazoo counties had their applications canceled. Aside from Holmes County, Sumner County had the best record of patenting: all three homesteaders received

31. All observations are based on the sample.

patents. Next was Jasper, where eleven of the twelve homesteaders received patents (seven white, three black, and one unknown). Aside from Copiah, Wilkinson, and Yazoo, Choctaw County had the worst record with thirteen out of fifteen cancellations. All of the known applicants were white.

The Southern Homestead Act allowed women to become homesteaders. Even so, overwhelming numbers of applicants were males. From the sample, it is calculated that there were 1,092 female and 7,705 male applicants, or 12.41 percent and 87.59 percent, respectively. Also, it is estimated that 14.56 percent of all women patented their homesteads. (See Appendix A, Tables 16–17.) In the sample, Lauderdale holds the distinction of having the largest percentage of women applicants—25.7 percent.

Tables 18 and 19 in Appendix A describe the age data of the homesteaders. The average age in the sample was about thirty-seven at the time of application. This varied only slightly by race. Blacks were about thirty-nine when they applied for land, and whites were thirty-six. The oldest person was seventy-two, and that person was white; the youngest was nineteen. The oldest black applicant was sixty-six years old.

Acreage data are the most complete, since this information is recorded on every application and final certificate. As noted, the average for all applications is known to be 86.2 acres. Slightly different figures appear for the sample. (See the data in Table 20 of Appendix A.) Overall, the sample average was 91.7 acres. For the smaller subsample of race-identified applicants, blacks' homesteads averaged 97.2 acres and whites', 96.4 acres.

It would be erroneous and impossible to project these findings on the rest of the South; however, some accurate figures are available on which to base some comparisons. The annual figures for original homestead applications exist. These include the total acreage in each state, the total public land acreage, as well as the number and acreage of original homestead applications. Discrepancies exist from one source to another, but they are not significant.

As Table 4 indicates, about 67,600 entries were made under the

TABLE 4
Original Homestead Applications

State	*Applications*	*Acreage*	*Homestead Average Size*
Alabama	16,284	1,546,569.0	95.0
Arkansas	26,395	2,367,889.9	89.7
Florida	9,675	968,195.4	100.1
Louisiana	6,452	748,281.7	115.8
Mississippi	8,797	758,460.9	86.2
	67,603	6,389,396.9	94.5

SOURCE: Appendix B, Tables 22 and 23.

Southern Homestead Act, comprising about 6.4 million acres. The average size of a homestead was 94.5 acres.[32]

It is instructive, however, to look closer at those figures—to break them down, for example, to determine if there is a considerable difference in the amount of land entered after 1868, when the 80-acre restriction expired. Before then, in fiscal 1867 and 1868, the average size of a homestead in the South was 67.7 acres. Homesteads in Louisiana came closest to the maximum allowable size with an average of 77.9 acres. Those figures change substantially for the period 1869 to 1876, when the average size of a homestead increased by almost 35 acres to 100.1. Louisiana again had the largest homesteads, averaging just over 117.6 acres. What is most interesting, though, is that the average did not even approach the maximum figure of 160 acres. The tremendous difference between the average size and the maximum allowed points to the inescapable conclusion that the southern public lands could not support

32. See Tables 22 and 23 of Appendix B for breakdown of all the figures. The three sources that were compared and used to supplement one another were the quarterly reports of the local officers to the GLO, Division "M," RG 49; Paul Gates, *History of the Public Land Law Development*, 335, 398, and 445 (his figures come from the GLO *Annual Reports*); and Thomas C. Donaldson, *The Public Domain: Its History with Statistics, to June 30 and December 1, 1883* (Washington, D.C., 1884).

very big farms. Land quality was, undoubtedly, a major factor in homestead size. Only 13.8 percent of the over 46 million acres of available public lands was entered. Arkansas had the most entries. (See Appendix B, Tables 22 and 23.)

The number of original entries does not tell the whole story; it is the amount of land patented that completes the picture. The figures become especially troublesome, for the number of final homestead certificates under the Southern Homestead Act is impossible to determine. Final homestead figures are available yearly. A settler had between five and seven years to make final proof, which meant homesteads made in 1876 could be "proved up" as late as 1883. But the final homestead figures for 1882 and 1883 could include homesteads made after June 30, 1876. That, of course, will inflate the numbers—but not too much, because only two years are involved.

Still, some estimates might be made. Table 5 shows that the GLO patented 27,800 claims, totaling about 2.9 million acres, about 106 acres per farm.

These figures mean that about 6 percent of all the public land was proved up. The final-patent figure of 27,800 means that about 41 percent of those who applied for land actually got title to it. That percentage is, of course, too high because of the inflated figure.

TABLE 5
Final Proof

State	*Titles*	*Percentage of Original Entries*	*Acreage*	*Homestead Average Size*
Alabama	6,293	38.6	720,773.3	114.5
Arkansas	12,680	48.0	1,259,646.8	99.3
Florida	4,072	42.1	443,904.4	109.0
Louisiana	2,373	36.8	285,729.1	120.4
Mississippi	2,382	27.1	236,014.7	99.1
	27,800	41.1	2,946,068.3	106.0

SOURCE: Appendix B, Tables 24 and 25.

The aggregate numbers reveal information that individual cases do not. Despite the dangers of using faulty records as the basis for estimates, the statistics do give a general picture of the homesteader. Coupled with the qualitative information for both black and white homesteaders, the numbers help complete the story.

V

The Erosion of the Southern Homestead Act

The Republican party, the party of emancipation and civil and voting rights for black people, was not going to attract many conservative white southerners, particularly former Confederates, who were long-time Democrats, and poor whites, who tended to be more Negrophobic than any other southerners. But Republicans would have to attract some of these people in order to make headway in the South. More specifically, some Republican leaders knew that white southerners had to be a factor in any program designed to achieve the agrarian ideal of a nation of small producers. There was hope. The Republican party also stood for prosperity and economic progress. Republicans had capital, and some Yankees who began moving south after the war had already shown that they were willing to invest that capital in southern economic development. Southerners were very much interested in the revitalization of their devastated and capital-poor region. And here was the point where the two paths could converge. By stressing the "gospel of prosperity," Republicans and Democrats, particularly the Whiggish Democrats, could agree on a program that would benefit both parties and the section as a whole. Leaders of the Conservative forces held the reins of financial power, and Republicans could execute their policies by appealing to Conservative economic interests. To put it differently, the economic part of the Republican program would help Conservatives ignore the equal rights part.

For Republicans, there was no conflict between the cultivation of

Conservative support for their economic program and the protection of the civil rights of black people. In fact, the two coincided. Eric Foner says the Republican attitude toward blacks was a part of the party's larger free labor ideology. In his words, "The Republicans' affirmation of the Negro's natural rights included the right to participate as a free laborer in the marketplace."[1] Particularly in state politics, this formulation provided Republicans the channels through which to build political power.

These disparate programs worked in political theory, but practical politics and social realities soon uncovered some basic contradictions. As Reconstruction proceeded, Republicans found that the building of power through the cultivation of former rebels meant the virtual abandonment of blacks. The economic program had been a means to build the type of society Republicans wanted, with new ideas, at least for the South, about wealth and labor. In the 1850s, the vision of populating the South with small farmers, each working his own acres, promised the alleviation of poverty, the destruction of large plantations, and the removal of control of southern politics from the hands of the planter oligarchy. But that vision ultimately failed because the Republicans concentrated more on the economic aspects of their policy, which promised more in terms of political power, than on the achievement of equality. Mark W. Summers, the historian of southern railroads during Reconstruction, interprets this emphasis as a betrayal of Republican ideals and a loss of the sense of mission that had characterized the party until the late 1860s. Eric Foner sees the party as limited because of its "flawed attitudes" concerning the Negro people and its "incomplete version" of the "full commitment" necessary for achieving the vision encompassed by their free labor ideology.[2]

The Southern Homestead Act was an obvious product of the Republican party's free labor ideology. Its architects, supporters, and

1. Eric Foner, *Free Soil,* 296.

2. Mark W. Summers, *Railroads, Reconstruction, and the Gospel of Prosperity: Aid under the Radical Republicans, 1865–1877* (Princeton, 1984), 157–60; Foner, *Free Soil,* 299–300. See also Michael Perman, *The Road to Redemption: Southern Politics, 1869–1879* (Chapel Hill, 1984).

detractors saw it as the way by which poor, landless persons, black and white, could own land. Because it required that federal lands be subject only to homesteading, it was a pure statement of the homestead principle. Put another way, the Southern Homestead Act embodied the agrarian ideal.

Yet, not all public land was available for settlement. Some of it was restricted by the legislation itself; for example, lands that contained minerals were excluded. Federal reservations, lands that had been classified as swamplands subject to transfer to the states, and grants to railroads were all off limits. Much public land was virtually closed to settlers due to its poor quality or because of problems in making it cultivable. Vast stands of timber covered much of the southern public lands, and although these acres were open for settlement, the difficulties and costs made homesteading impractical.

These lands might not appear to be important, at least insofar as homesteaders were concerned. However, the railroad lands and the timberlands demonstrate, more than anything else, the contradictions in Republican party ideology. The Southern Homestead Act was a perfect symbol of the party's free labor ideology, and the railroad and timberlands represent its emphasis on economic development. In a larger context, the contrast is one between the agrarian ideal and the realities of local and regional development. On the one hand, the ownership of property was the means of support for a democratic citizenry and ultimately the foundation of the Republic; on the other, the development of the region could proceed faster and more widely in the control of persons and companies with money to invest. The conflict also represented the beginning of the end of the Southern Homestead Act.

The railroad lands were grants of federal lands in odd-numbered sections to the states for the construction of railroads; the alternate even-numbered sections were open for homesteading. Most of these grants were made in the 1850s, with a ten-year statute of limitations on them. In other words, grants were contingent upon beginning construction within ten years. Since little or no construction had been done because of the war, forfeitures came due at about the same time the Southern Homestead Act became law, and the way Congress handled the matter tells a great deal about party politics.

Until Congress determined the status of the odd-numbered sections, the GLO decided to do nothing with them. The even-numbered sections continued to be regarded as double-minimum land, according to the original terms of the grants. This meant the cash value of the land was double the minimum price, that is, $2.50 an acre, and only half the usual amount could be claimed, namely, forty-acre tracts until 1868, and then eighty-acre tracts.[3]

The expiration of the grants did not go unnoticed by land-hungry settlers, and Louisianians were just as eager to get railroad lands as were any other southerners. Juste Bertinot summed up the hopes and fears of many when he wrote the commissioner from Grand Coteau: "In relation to R.R. lands in Louisiana, many persons are anxious to Settle upon them, and as the Crops are promising and hence will have . . . money, they would like to take advantage of the Homestead law and have a plantation of their own, but those persons are afraid to do so through false reports that the Government will not give them a patent." Some settled anyway and found out those reports were not false at all.[4]

Radicals in Congress believed that the forfeitures should be implemented immediately. For one thing, loss of property would be a way of punishing rebels; for another, forfeiture would make land, much of it very good acreage, available to actual settlers. George Julian believed the original grants were wrongheaded anyway, that they led to monopolization of the soil and were therefore "repugnant to republican government." Accordingly, he attempted to get legislation to confirm the forfeitures and open the land to settlement. In early December, 1867, a House committee produced H.R.

3. R&R, Montgomery, to J. M. Edmunds, June 5, 1866, in MLR, G–80024; Edmunds to R&R, Montgomery, June 18, 1866, in Letters Sent. The Montgomery officers had requested information on the railroad grants because persons were applying for land in the odd-numbered sections.

4. Juste Bertinot to Wilson, August 28, 1868, in MLR, H–42094; Bertinot to Wilson, September 14, 1868, in MLR, H–43290.

267, which received extensive consideration in late January and early February, 1868. It passed the House, but the Senate Public Lands Committee reported it adversely in February, 1869, and the measure died.[5]

The main provision of the bill was simple. Lands granted to Alabama, Mississippi, Louisiana, and Florida in 1856 for railroad construction and not lawfully disposed of, about five million acres, were forfeited and "henceforward [made] subject to homestead entry and settlement" under the Southern Homestead Act.[6]

Congressmen favoring the bill supported five main arguments. Julian made the first point when he told why the lands were forfeited: "The inexcusable failure of the States to comply with the conditions of the grant," and "their acts of treason and rebellion against the Government." Put differently, the measure was an act of punishment, or, stated positively, the purpose was to open the lands to homesteading "for the relief of the homeless loyal poor of the South who are hungering and thirsting for their just rights."[7]

Joseph McClurg of Missouri, chairman of the Committee on Southern Railroads, went even further. Pointing his finger at those connected with southern railroads, he noted that the railroads were controlled by rebels. McClurg's committee was in the process of collecting testimony on the southern roads, and although all the facts were not yet in, McClurg was sure about one thing: "In no case [had] the stockholders either North or South protested against the use of the roads in aid of the rebellion or even remonstrated." The interim secretary of war had reported his own observations to McClurg's committee: "In almost every case the management of the roads had been closely identified with the initiation of rebellion, and had contributed to sustain it against the Government, both by

5. George W. Julian, "Our Land Policy," *Atlantic Monthly,* XLIII (March, 1879), 334; *Congressional Globe,* 40th Cong., 1st Sess., 225, 615–17.

6. H.R. 267, *A Bill to Declare Forfeited to the United States Certain Lands Granted to Aid in the Construction of Railroads in the States of Alabama, Mississippi, Louisiana, and Florida, and for other Purposes,* 40th Cong., 2nd Sess., 1867. Arkansas received no grants in 1856.

7. *Congressional Globe,* 40th Cong., 2nd Sess., 310–11, 695.

the influence and means of the companies. During the war they had followed the fortunes of the bastard government with a zeal most commendable had it been in a worthy cause, but most contemptible and criminal, being manifested in the cause of treason." Benjamin F. Butler, erstwhile commander in New Orleans, confirmed the disloyalty of the railroads in Louisiana during the war. He told his colleagues that the New Orleans, Opelousas, and Great Western had about eighty miles of completed track between New Orleans and Berwick Bay and would have remained useless except that, as Butler put it, "one of my staff stood on the engine with a revolver at [the engineer's] head."[8]

A third argument is closely related to the first two and to the traditional thinking that pitted individual landownership against monopoly and speculation. According to this perspective the aristocracy of the South was responsible for the treasonable behavior of the section; these same people controlled the southern railroad companies. Forfeiture of these grants of federal land would make them available for settlement, thereby placing landowners among monopolists and weakening the stranglehold of the handful of capitalists.

No one pointed his finger at the South more accusingly than the congressman from Pennsylvania, William Kelley. He explained just how these "corporators" schemed to increase their revenues at the expense of the actual settler: "The original grantees did not mean to build roads. . . . This magnificent grant was made to corporators who did not expect to construct roads, but meant to hold the grants for seven, eight, or nine years during which the lands would, by the energy and enterprise of others, increase in value immensely, and then to sell them to those who would construct the roads provided for in the act." He summarized his view when he said, "The contest over this bill is a struggle between rebel land speculators and the loyal people of the South, white and black. . . . It is a question . . . between labor and capital."[9]

8. *Ibid.*, 813–14, 695, 311.
9. *Ibid.*, 870–71.

The Fortieth Congress considered a fourth argument not debated in Congress before, namely, the condition of the federal lands. Supporters of the railroad forfeitures argued that many of the grants were on superior lands and should, therefore, be made available to settlers rather than to corporations. Julian said that the five million acres in question were "rich Lands" and that those available under the Southern Homestead Act were "worthless for tillage and failed to find purchasers prior to the war." Kelley picked Florida to dramatize the need for the railroad lands:

> Bacon said, "Sand has always its roots in clay; and there be no veins of sand in great depth within the earth." But he had not seen Florida. . . . The seventeen million acres open to settlement in Florida do not contain a forty-acre homestead of arable land. It is sand, sand, sand, deep as the bottom of the ocean, proving that there is an exception to Bacon's maxim as there is to every general rule. Peninsular Florida is a mere bed of sand washed out by the ocean and left there, and the gentleman, with his hardy eastern energy, could not pluck from forty acres of it enough to maintain his little family.

Governor Marvin supported Kelley's claims with perhaps one of the greatest overstatements in Florida history: "No well can be dug or made. It must and will, through countless centuries, remain an arid waste."[10] Kelley's purpose was to get Congress to add lands of better quality to the public domain.

The last argument in favor of the bill elaborated on the special needs of the freedmen. Kelley and others repeated the often-expressed view that the freedmen must learn to take care of themselves and that landownership would provide the means. The best way, he felt, to "make the freedom" promised by the Emancipation Proclamation, the Civil Rights Act, and other legislation was to open "the only fertile land available for present settlement" in the four states covered by the railroad bill. John Shanks of Indiana explained that the four million black people of the South must have land, because "every nation is weakened when its citizens have no homes."[11]

10. *Ibid.*, 310, 695, 871.
11. *Ibid.*, 872, 973, 977.

The bill's detractors answered all these arguments, except the one dealing with land quality. Most opponents of forfeiture were Democrats, but it is revealing that a few Republicans were willing to break party ranks and oppose the bill. Consideration of this measure came relatively early in "Radical" Reconstruction, and Mark Summers has shown that many Republicans, particularly at the state level, favored aid for railroads and were able to attract Democratic support. Yet, if that aid was to be in the form of federal lands, Republicans had doubts. For example, some in Mississippi voted against any surrender of the public domain to railroads, believing it to be a betrayal of Republican principle. In one instance in the early 1870s, the Mississippi House petitioned Congress for a land grant to a particular railroad; twenty-six Republicans and one Democrat voted against the appeal.[12]

The opposition strongly believed the bill would injure northern capital investments and that loyal people in the South would suffer. Fernando Wood, Democrat of New York, told his fellow members early in the debate that probably three-quarters of the capital of all southern railroads built since 1856 came from New York, Boston, or Philadelphia. His ire was obvious: "The object of this resolution is to confiscate northern capital, to apply a rule to northern capital because it is invested in the southern States which has not been applied to railroads in the West." When questioned about the source of his information, Wood could not supply it. Indiana's John Coburn, a Republican, differed with Wood. The testimony he had heard convinced him that "much of the stock was owned in the South." For example, the city of New Orleans owned two-thirds of the New Orleans, Opelousas, and Great Western.[13]

James G. Blaine, moderate Republican from Maine, believed it was fruitless to discuss who controlled the roads during the war. Now they were in the hands of loyal men, so the grants should stand. Democrat John Chanler of New York, one of the most vociferous

12. Summers, *Railroads*, 72.

13. *Congressional Globe*, 40th Cong., 1st Sess., 616; *Congressional Globe*, 40th Cong., 2nd Sess., 842.

opponents of the bill, argued that the bill was "special legislation, discriminating between classes to the general injury of the whole country. And on that general ground I am opposed to the bill." His view was similar to that held by Republican and Democratic promoters in the South who believed that railroads would benefit the entire region, not just the areas through which the rails ran.[14]

Several congressmen believed the bill to be unfair to the South because it deprived the section of some grants held in good faith. Chanler said that the bill ignored those roads that were almost completed and undermined the welfare of the South by undercutting loyalty. Democrat Samuel B. Axtell of California, in speaking of the New Orleans, Opelousas, and Great Western, argued that the government betrayed American values when it attempted to revoke grants where work was completed, and asked the country "to pause before giving this emphatic notice that they [the South] will call in vain on us to renew the grants after they have invested their money and completed large portions of the roads."[15]

Some congressmen, emphasizing reconciliation of the sections, argued against forfeiture. Axtell believed the easiest way to recultivate "mutual friendships, interests, and esteem" was through an easy communication network, so the southern states must be allowed to continue building their railroads.[16]

Opponents also indirectly addressed the issue of the need for land for the former slaves. Democrat Charles Eldridge of Wisconsin was convinced that Julian ultimately intended to subject the white man "to the supremacy and domination of the African." Democrat William Mungen refused to believe that black people could care for themselves. He baldly asserted, "God in His inscrutable providence made the negro what he is, always has been, and always will be—

14. *Congressional Globe,* 40th Cong., 2nd Sess., 809–10; Paul Gates, "Federal Land Policy in the South," 308, says that Blaine had business and railroad interests. See also Summers, *Railroads,* Parts 1 and 2 *passim.*

15. *Congressional Globe,* 40th Cong., 2nd Sess., 808, 834–35. At the time of his death, Axtell was counsel for the Southern Pacific Railroad.

16. *Congressional Globe,* 40th Cong., 2nd Sess., 835–36.

inferior to the white man; just as he made the vulture inferior to the eagle."[17]

H.R. 267 passed the House of Representatives on February 5, 1868. The vote was 86 to 73, with 30 members not voting. The Democrats almost unanimously opposed the bill; the sole Democrat voting yea was William Holman, Julian's colleague from Indiana. The Republicans were divided. Although a majority (85) favored it, almost 40 percent (56) either voted no (33) or chose not to vote (23). Significantly and more to the point, the Republican consensus did not hold when economic matters were linked to Reconstruction issues.[18]

The faithful of the Republican party did not let this considerable desertion go unnoticed. William Kelley put words into the mouths of laboring men of the country: "You, Republicans, who claim to be the friends of equal rights, in our hour of suffering, when thousands of the most industrious of us are without employment, shut us out from five million acres of fertile land available for homesteads and give it to the wealthiest rebels of the South." George Julian told of northern Republicans who moved South, supposedly to help the freedmen. Instead these Yankees became embroiled in railroad speculation in Louisiana and, in the end, opposed the granting of lands to homeless blacks. He recounted how officers commanding the Colored Troops would often "dissuade their men from going upon homesteads" and induce them to work for planters instead. The officers would receive money for each man they sent back to the plantation.[19]

The question of railroad forfeiture never got past the Senate. The Committee on Public Lands reported it adversely because, it said, it did not want to act until the South was represented. The committee also believed that it would be unfair to pass a general law without

17. *Ibid.*, 971–72.

18. *Ibid.*, 985. The thirty-three nays included the following: thirteen from New England; nine from the mid-Atlantic states; two from Tennessee; three from Missouri; two from Michigan; two from Iowa; and one each from West Virginia and Nebraska.

19. *Congressional Globe*, 40th Cong., 2nd Sess., 807, 871.

judging each railroad on its own merits. In July, 1870, a bill dealing specifically with forfeiture of the lands in the New Orleans, Opelousas, and Great Western Railroad grant passed both houses. Hundreds of people settled on the lands, but two years later, they were still waiting for confirmation of their claims. Until the governor prepared a list of those lands, all claims and counterclaims were held in abeyance.[20]

In the case of the railroad lands, some Republicans tried to provide more and better land to southern homesteaders, but Democrats had blocked the effort. As time went on, railroads received less and less aid, particularly in the form of federal lands, not because Republicans believed that their original grants were wrong and that settlers should have the land, though this was important, but because the promised returns never materialized. On the state level, the coalition of Republicans and Democrats, welded together by the gospel of prosperity, fell apart by the early 1870s. That part of the Reconstruction program was doomed to failure, at least for the time being. The Southern Homestead Act was still viable legislation in the 1870s, but the failure of the forfeitures created difficulties for homesteaders already settled on the railroad grants, and certainly for those eager to move there.

The conflict of timber interest with southern public land policy provides an unmatched example of how larger development concerns clashed with the agrarian ideal. It also points up important issues in the formulation of public land policy. Whether intentional or not, the men who wrote the homestead laws made no major distinctions about land use, and the heavily timbered lands are a good example of the problem. Persons or business concerns could move onto these lands, file homestead claims, strip the valuable timber, and then move on. They were breaking the law because these

20. *Congressional Globe,* 40th Cong., 3rd Sess., 1364. The bill was H.R. 2359, *Congressional Globe,* 41st Cong., 2nd Sess., 5128, 5314, 5657; Thomas T. Tolson to G. W. Julian, February 6, 1872, in MLR, I–82377. The lands were finally opened in early 1873. See Andrew Hero to Commissioner, February 15, 1873, in MLR, K–36068, in which he enclosed the list of lands clipped from a newspaper, and GLO to R&R, New Orleans, October 9, 1874, in Letters Sent.

particular lands were set aside for settlement. It was common practice to break the law, and there was no effective machinery to enforce it.[21]

The Southern Homestead Act did not exclude from settlement the federal timberlands. That encouraged fraud. No other crime was perpetrated against the southern public lands more often than illegal applications for the purpose of securing the timber. That is to say, public land policy encouraged extensive timber depredation. The GLO, aware of this problem, supported legislation exempting the timberlands from the Southern Homestead Act. The legislation, however, was never altered, and so people found ways to circumvent it.[22]

Escambia County, Alabama, suffered extensive depredation. When someone contested a claim there because no one had moved onto it within the required six months, evidence proved that the claim was made solely to strip the timber. In federal circuit court, the judge dismissed the case, saying that a person who claimed land could do what he wanted with it.[23]

George W. Mann, a Civil War veteran with a real estate business in Hot Springs, Arkansas, applied for a homestead in the Camden district in the fall of 1873. He began building a one-story house and removing the timber for further settlement and cultivation. He also built a saw mill. The commissioner of the GLO decided not to allow him to have the land because, he said, "the erection of a saw mill on the premises indicates that the timber is being manufactured into lumber for speculative rather than domestic purposes." Mann was also subject to criminal prosecution for trespassing on the public lands.[24]

21. See Robbins, *Our Landed Heritage*, 245.

22. Willis Drummond to W. P. Kellogg, February 13, 1872, Samuel Burdett to George S. Boutwell, January 30, 1875, in Division "C," Letters Sent to Members of Congress. He also supported the sale of timber lands in the *Annual Report* (1874), 5–7, 40–41. It will be recalled that in 1866 the Senate tried to adopt an amendment to the southern homestead bill that would have excluded timber and mineral lands from the provisions. In the final act, only the mineral lands were excluded.

23. Stearns and Somerville to Commissioner, June 22, 1876, in MLR, M–12644.

24. GLO to R&R, Camden, December 20, 1875, in Letters Sent.

Florida reported extensive depredation. Joseph Valentine, a black deputy timber agent for Hamilton, Madison, and Suwannee counties, could not keep up with the lawbreakers. The Suwannee River was "filled" for miles "with logs recently cut." He also noted the impossibility of distinguishing between federal and state timber. But Valentine's report is more significant for the public reaction to the swindling: the people "either from interest or fear" would not give him any information. He continued, "Almost the entire population seem to be under the influence and patronage of the proprietors of the immense mills run in that neighborhood. [A]s timber Agent I found no Sympathy in my work. Although the depredations and depredators no doubt are well known to the community generally I found very few who were willing to give me any information that would aid me in finding stolen timber." Why the public refused to cooperate must remain unclear. One reason might have been Valentine's own reluctance to pursue the matter. The man he stayed with while conducting his research reported that Valentine went out to investigate only one day. "He seemed to be afraid to venture out & attend to his business, saying he was afraid some of the trespassers would kill him."[25]

One citizen in the county reported that lumber mills were hiring freedmen to homestead land so the companies could have the timber. Thus, both the government and blacks were being cheated. A special agent with the Post Office believed that most of these Florida lumbermen were "Rebels of the worst stripe who think it a great feat and an honor to rob from the Government." He also reported that these companies were supplying railroad ties for the New York Central, Penn Central, York and Erie, and Southern Pacific railroads.[26] These "Rebels" seemed to be willing not only to cooperate with their former enemies for economic gain, but also to break the law to do so.

25. Joseph Valentine, first report, July 19, 1873, enclosed in letter of John Banks and S. F. Halliday to R&R, Gainesville, August 20, 1873, in MLR, K–65144; William Page to Commissioner, November 28, 1873, in MLR, K–78194.

26. William Page to R&R, Tallahassee, June 8, 1873, in MLR, K–58045; Leib to "Curtis," June 3, 1873, in MLR, K–53142; Leib to GLO, June 27, 1873, in MLR, K–56843.

Louisiana's swamps and forests did not escape depredation. John E. Hudson took out a homestead to obtain cypress timber to build railroad crossties. The informant who betrayed Hudson was convinced Hudson's action was fraudulent, "for no man can settle upon the land he entered, neither cattle of any description can range thereon. It is beyond the reclamation of man, being an immense cypress swamp, subject to tidle overflows from Lake Maurepas and the river Tangipaho."[27]

New Orleans Register John Breaux and Receiver Julian Neville provided a very detailed account of how they dealt with public timber depredations. They confirmed reports coming from St. Tammany Parish north of Lake Pontchartrain, but their hands were tied because of lack of funds. So they decided that, as timber agents for the district, they would seize the lumber as it came into the market and personally oversee its sale in New Orleans. The accused parties claimed that the timber had been cut on private lands, and they were able to get an order from the U.S. Circuit Court enjoining the local officers from proceeding with the sale.

Breaux and Neville made some efforts to remedy the problem. They hoped more forceful execution of the law would result from a requirement that their deputies be paid from the sale of timber they seized. But the plan was not successful; the depredation continued.

The U.S. district attorney hindered their efforts at vigorous prosecution. The officers had construed the law to mean that landowners must prove that the timber had not been cut from federal lands; but the district attorney ruled that the local officers must assume the burden of proof. This, of course, meant dealing with the frustrating problem of finding witnesses to testify against the depredators. In the end, the local officers were exasperated and felt defeated by the government's policies.[28]

The pattern of depredations was the same in Mississippi. In 1871, a citizen reported that persons applying for lands around Columbia

27. John M. Bach to Wilson, March 25, 1870, in MLR, H–96574.

28. This entire account is taken from the letter of Breaux and Neville to Commissioner, June 20, 1876, in MLR, M–12454.

meant only to cut the timber, and that freedmen were being "induced" to homestead "by some white persons" who acquired the timber on the freedmen's homesteads "at low rates."[29]

Protecting the heavily timbered public lands and enforcing the timber policy of the United States taxed the resources of local officers, mainly because of the lack of machinery to protect and prosecute. The laws governing the preservation of federal timber were at least twenty years old. An 1831 law, which made depredations a criminal offense punishable by fine and imprisonment, provided no real protective machinery, so enforcement was negligible. In 1855, Congress authorized the General Land Office to supervise and protect the timber on the public lands. This responsibility rested with the local land officers, making them timber agents whose job it was to make reports, initiate proceedings against offenders, and collect fees for the use of the timber on the public lands. These duties exacerbated the already overburdened southern officers, so Congress provided some relief in 1872 when it authorized appropriations for deputy timber agents. Now the registers and receivers could hire people to help them enforce the laws. Not until the late 1870s, when Carl Schurz became secretary of the interior, did conservation become established as a principle in American land policy.[30]

Numerous cries for assistance poured into Washington, some going so far as to demand the military take care of the problem. The local officers reported that Escambia County, Alabama, was a dangerous place, because "individuals who should attempt to seize and protect the Timber . . . would be killed." The U.S. marshal could find no men to hire at the government price "*nor at any price,* to risk their lives in the business." As a result, the land officers contended that "nothing short of an adequate military force will stop those

29. W. H. B. Lane to Commissioner, October 16, 1871, in MLR, I–68372. For another, later example, see R. T. Aston to GLO, n.d. (received July 6, 1874), in MLR, L–9348.

30. Robbins, *Our Landed Heritage,* 241; Harold H. Dunham, "Government Handout: A Study in the Administration of the Public Lands 1875–1891" (Ph.D. dissertation, Columbia University, 1941), 48, 50–51. Congress authorized the fees in 1864.

extensive depredations." The local land officers in New Orleans reported that "at least three deputy surveyors have lost their lives" in the southwest corner of the state.[31] Frontier violence was very much alive—particularly on the southern federal lands.

While some agents found it impossible to do their jobs, others did not even try. Some accepted the appointments for the pay, which was not very much anyway; others worked on the side of the lumbermen. In 1878, the Cincinnati *Daily Enquirer* did a story on some of the timber agents in Florida during Grant's administration. The paper reported that all B. F. Livingston did was draw his salary; he did not even know where the timber was. Henry Clews knew nothing about the public domain and "did not try to find out"; he accepted the job only to collect the pay. Isadore Bloomenthat, collector of customs at Cedar Keys, claimed that he knew all the Florida agents and that their appointments were "political positions and sinecures." They did not work because it was not expected of them.[32]

Thomas B. Scully, an agent for the New Orleans district, was accused of "compromising" with the lumbermen and selling the timber on government lands. When the commissioner found out about it, he scolded the local officers and told them they were to hire "none but *trustworthy persons*" as deputies. One Louisianian believed that inadequate pay accounted for corruption. If that was so, encouraging the New Orleans officers to protect the timber was "equivalent to lisensing them to levy black mail on those thieves." Then, in a telling indictment against Louisiana public officials, he said of the register and receiver: "I know them personally to be as pure as the average Louisiana official."[33]

Depredation was an extremely serious problem, and agents who believed that their jobs were political sinecures, who actively cooperated with the depredators, or who turned their heads the other

31. Stearns and Moore to Drummond, September 30, 1871, in MLR, I–81752; Lott and Neville to Drummond, November 28, 1873, enclosing report of Mathew Rowe, November 12, 1873, in MLR, K–77887.

32. Cincinnati *Daily Enquirer*, April 3, 1878.

33. GLO to R&R, New Orleans, September 9, 1874, in Letters Sent; John E. Leet to Commissioner Williamson, July 17, 1876, in MLR, M–17089.

way did not help to alleviate the destruction. Clearly, they encouraged the depredations, because as newer portions of the South opened for settlement, profits made from clearing land, selling lumber, or providing wood for railroad construction simply multiplied. Because the Southern Homestead Act restricted all federal lands to settlement, the illegal and fraudulent claims made by these men hastened the erosion of the act.

Public lands along the Calcasieu River in southwestern Louisiana provided new, rich sources of timber for exploitation. The surveyor general reported that public lands in Calcasieu Parish were being "rapidly" stripped of their "valuable Pine timber, for which they are so celebrated." The cut timber was rafted down the river to the saw mills in Lake Charles and from there shipped to Galveston and other Gulf ports for the construction of railroads. Local newspapers boasted of the size of the trade and the number of boats employed in it.[34]

Much of Mississippi's public land was heavily laden with timber, and for a small fee, a person could get 160 acres, make $1,000, and move on. The U.S. commissioner for southern Mississippi explained how depredation eroded the Southern Homestead Act: "Such a state of things does not make citizens because as soon as the Timber is cut they move off some where's else and the land is so poor that when once the timber is cut no person will purchase it for anything. Men having a large capital are now and have been for some years past engaged in cutting timber."[35]

By 1874, several southern congressmen responded to the problem. Republican Representative Frank Morey of Louisiana introduced legislation to make southern public lands subject to the same laws that applied everywhere else. In other words, his bill would repeal the provision of the Southern Homestead Act that restricted southern lands only to homesteading.[36]

34. Barnard and Hyatt to Drummond, May 2, 1871, enclosing letter of E. W. Foster to Barnard and Hyatt of May 1, 1871, in MLR, I–46748.

35. John E. Sweeney to Commissioner, May 19, 1870, in MLR, I–3178.

36. *Congressional Record,* 43rd Cong., 1st Sess., 4633.

Omar Conger of Michigan, also a Republican, strongly opposed the measure. He lamented that settling the poor on the land and preventing speculation—so crucial in 1866—no longer counted as a high priority. Morey replied that the South wanted to be treated like the rest of the states, having "passed out of the condition of tutelage." He told Conger that the homestead laws were irrelevant to timberlands. Morey argued that the only way to obtain timberland under the present legislation was to steal it.[37]

The argument finally came back to the freedmen again. Conger affirmed that because the federal government had a responsibility to protect the freedmen, special legislation for the South was necessary. Morey then presented a petition from Calcasieu and Cameron parishes, claiming that four-fifths of the signers were black. They demanded a change in the laws. Conger would not budge. He said that he represented lumber interests in Michigan, who were at that moment waiting in Florida, Louisiana, and Arkansas for the bill to pass. But he would not support them.[38]

Neither side got its way. Morey had the bill recommitted because the opposition was using tactics to delay its passage. But southerners had begun their campaign to change the law. Two years later, victory would come, and timber and speculative interests contributed to the repeal of the Southern Homestead Act.

37. *Ibid.*, 4633–34.
38. *Ibid.*, 4634.

VI

Repeal: The Circle Comes Complete

On June 22, 1876, exactly ten years after it was passed, Congress in effect repealed the Southern Homestead Act. Two factors help explain the enactment of the repeal legislation: the quality of the public lands and the winding down of Reconstruction.

On December 7, 1875, Senator Powell Clayton of Arkansas introduced Senate Bill 2 to repeal Section 2303 of the Revised Statutes of the United States, the section that reserved all of the public domain in the five southern public land states for homesteading.[1] Since this provision was the only one governing the southern public lands, its repeal would destroy the Southern Homestead Act. The arguments over the bill were not new. The Southern Homestead Act discriminated against the South. The poor quality of the southern lands made the homesteading-only provision meaningless. The Southern Homestead Act retarded the economic development of the region. On the other side, those who opposed repeal clung tenaciously to the view that revocation would effectively deny the freedmen the opportunity of owning land and would encourage speculation.

In his opening remarks, Powell Clayton summarized the hardships that the Southern Homestead Act inflicted upon the South. Settlers who would rather pay cash and obtain title immediately could not do so; they had to homestead. The act encouraged lumber mill owners to make fraudulent homestead applications. The lands

1. *Congressional Record*, 44th Cong., 1st Sess., 185.

were poor for farms but valuable for timber, and the southern states would realize much revenue if the Southern Homestead Act was repealed. Finally, the law was unfair because, as Clayton put it, "all congressional legislation which deprives the citizens of one State from the exercise of privileges which the citizens of other States under similar circumstances are permitted to enjoy is vicious."[2]

Senator Charles Jones, a Democrat from Florida, underscored the fairness issue. When Florida was admitted to the Union in 1845, the state agreed not to tax the public lands, provided that the federal government would pay to Florida 5 percent of the proceeds from their sale, this money to be used for educational purposes. The Southern Homestead Act changed all that: because the public lands in Florida could not be sold, there was no federal money for education.[3]

Jones also demonstrated that the Southern Homestead Act discouraged immigration of entrepreneurs and encouraged trespassers. He summed up the arguments for the preachers of the New South gospel:

> [Florida] is filling up with enterprising gentlemen from the North and from the East and from the West, gentlemen who have been reared in the lumber business, who are acquainted with it; and we feel a very decided interest in the development of this great interest in our State. . . . [The lands] are only valuable for timber purposes; and under the present system the trespasser and the trespasser alone has the advantage. The honest man cannot go into the market and buy them. He who desires to make a permanent settlement cannot go there and get a title at once; but he has to sit down five years and take all the risks and contingencies incident to life before he can acquire title to any land in those States. In order to facilitate improvements and immigration we must have a system by which the settler can obtain at once a title to the land.[4]

Jones believed that land improvement and immigration would follow repeal. He heralded the approach of the New South.

Texan Samuel Maxey also believed the timber was being under-

2. *Ibid.*, 815.
3. *Ibid.*, 816.
4. *Ibid.*

utilized because of the homestead restriction. Although Texas had no federal lands, Maxey believed that the southern public land states would benefit from repeal. In this view, the law deprived the citizens of those states of their privileges and immunities guaranteed by the Fourteenth Amendment. Maxey also argued that the law was unconstitutional because it favored blacks. They should have neither more nor less than other citizens.[5]

James Alcorn of Mississippi also favored repeal, because the Southern Homestead Act had not delivered on its promises. "Congress in its mercy, so far as Mississippi is concerned, when these people [freedmen] held up their hands and asked for bread, gave them in return a pine lot in the form of a homestead law." He concluded, "So far as the colored people are concerned, so far as the poor of the State are concerned, the present law amounts to nothing."[6]

William Windom, a Republican from Minnesota, admitted that the 1866 law was a failure. That act was "a cover" for dishonesty and gave "a reward to perjury" because timber interests had to lie to acquire the lands. Repeal would prove lucrative, because the increased business due to the sale of the public lands would help provide funds to the empty coffers of the states. He also believed the poor would benefit because of the demand for more workers in manufacturing.[7]

Opponents also drew on old arguments. George F. Edmunds of Vermont believed that Congress had placed restrictions on the southern lands so freedmen would not be "crowded out" by public sales or preemption claims. Clayton responded by maintaining that his black colleague from Mississippi, Blanche K. Bruce, had carefully examined the bill for repeal and believed that it should pass. Bruce's support, Clayton hoped, would allay the fears of those concerned for the welfare of the black people.[8] Although there is no

5. *Ibid.*, 1089.
6. *Ibid.*, 850–51.
7. *Ibid.*, 852, 1087.
8. *Ibid.*, 817, 906.

direct statement from Bruce on the Southern Homestead Act, it is instructive to note that he was absent when the roll was called on final passage.

Edmunds feared, too, that opening the public lands to private sale would encourage speculation. To prevent this, he proposed an additional section, closing the public lands to private entry until they had been offered at public sale. The hope was that they could attract higher prices and bring more money into the federal treasury. Edmunds believed that the lands should not be subject to private entry "until in the altered condition of the country, with free labor everywhere and increasing populations in those [federal land] States, all the incentives to the increase of wealth growing out of the increase of these lands should be weighed."[9]

Clayton decided the only way around Edmunds was to offer a substitute to his amendment. It read: "That the public lands affected by this act shall be offered at public sale as soon as practicable, from time to time and according to the provisions of existing laws, and shall not be subject to private entry until they are so offered." As will be seen in the interpretation of this section, the amendment applied only to cash sales and not to homestead entries. The public auction, Clayton believed, would create more expenses to the government and "will delay somewhat the bringing of the lands into market," but his ultimate purpose—repeal of the Southern Homestead Act—would be accomplished.[10]

Allen Thurman of Ohio proposed another amendment to protect the rights, "complete or inchoate," of homesteaders who were already on the land. His purpose was "to prevent a man from entering on land on which a homestead settlement has already been made."[11] Both amendments were adopted.

Debate over the land's value was protracted. Many on both sides seemed to agree that much of the public domain was useless for homesteading and valuable for timber. But how to dispose of it for

9. *Ibid.*, 906.
10. *Ibid.*, 936.
11. *Ibid.*, 818.

the mutual benefit of the public treasury and the timber interests was at the heart of the controversy. The supporters of repeal got a welcome vote of encouragement from the commissioner of the General Land Office. He believed that the conditions which spawned the Southern Homestead Act no longer existed. He labeled it "unequal and obnoxious," much to the delight of southerners like Senator Jones of Florida. But aside from that, he believed that the timber was valuable and some particular regulations should continue to cover these lands, even to the point of excluding only the timberlands from homesteading—a provision in the original 1866 legislation which was subsequently removed before passage.[12]

One solution was Clayton's amendment—offering the lands at public sale before subjecting them to private entry. Another was to appraise the lands in each section prior to sale and ensure the timberlands would not sell for less than the minimum. This proposal, actually offered by Senator Boutwell of Massachusetts,[13] was simply the old suggestion to distinguish land types and land use in the public surveys.

Boutwell later offered another solution, a new one not considered before—conservation. He proposed that timberlands be offered for sale in 320-acre lots at not less than $1.25 an acre. The claimant had to remove the wood within three years and could not make another entry until he had done so. He also suggested that one tree per acre of every type growing there should be left standing. And all live oak and red cedar would be automatically reserved unless the president directed otherwise.[14] Conservation of the nation's natural resources was just beginning to become a national issue.

The bill to repeal the Southern Homestead Act passed the Senate on February 15, 1876, by a vote of 41 to 17. Fourteen members did not vote.[15] Of those voting, all the Democrats favored repeal. The Republicans, however, were clearly divided. While 38 percent

12. *Ibid.*, 852, 1090.
13. *Ibid.*, 937.
14. *Ibid.*, 1084.
15. *Ibid.*, 1090.

favored repeal, 41 percent did not; almost one-fifth of the Republicans did not vote, while about 15 percent of the Democrats did not. Most northeastern Republicans voted nay, and most southern and western Republicans voted yea.

The five public land states favored repeal. Florida's Democrat voted yes; the Republican was absent. Both of Alabama's senators favored repeal; one was a Democrat, the other a Republican. Both of Mississippi's senators were Republican; one was absent, the other voted yes. Louisiana's sole senator, a Republican, voted yes, and both of Arkansas' Republican senators favored repeal.[16]

The debate in the House echoed the one in the Senate. There was, for example, some concern about depriving black people of their opportunities to acquire homesteads. Hernando Money of Mississippi assured his colleagues that southerners wanted blacks to have land, but he also told them that the freedmen preferred to stay on the plantations. This was an obvious proplantation argument, but Representative Money believed that the poor quality of the public lands hindered settlement.[17]

Concern arose about timber and speculation. Goldsmith W. Hewitt of Alabama understood that some northerners opposed repeal because they feared that newer southern industry would threaten northern business concerns. Hewitt pointed out, for example, that iron interests in Pennsylvania had rivals in Alabama. Indiana coal interests opposed similar industries in Alabama. Michigan lumber interests feared lumbering in Alabama, Mississippi, and

16. These votes were as follows:

Florida:	Simon B. Conover (R)	ab
	Charles W. Jones (D)	yea
Alabama:	George Goldthwaite (D)	yea
	George E. Spencer (R)	yea
Mississippi:	James L. Alcorn (R)	yea
	Blanche K. Bruce (R)	ab
Louisiana:	J. Rodman West (R)	yea
Arkansas:	Powell Clayton (R)	yea
	Stephen W. Dorsey (R)	yea

17. *Congressional Record*, 44th Cong., 1st Sess., 3294.

Florida, and so on. In other words, arguing against repeal because it would encourage monopoly and speculation was hypocritical.[18]

The discussion of the South's future in this context would never have occurred if the public lands did not promise to provide a fertile setting for industrial development. Put differently, much of the land was not suited for agricultural purposes. House members, though, wanted to make some distinctions between lands that were suitable for homesteading and those that were not. This led to an early, sketchy discussion about land use. Representatives Hernando Money of Mississippi and William Holman of Indiana both proposed amendments that would have excluded from repeal lands suitable for agriculture. In other words, only agricultural lands were to be subject to the homestead laws.[19] Their amendments never passed, but they do suggest the concern of some for the proper allocation and utilization of the public domain.

Others wanted to go even further. At a time when southerners were trying to repeal the homesteading-only restriction, representatives from Iowa and Kansas advocated the extension of this restriction to the rest of the country. Proper land utilization was a factor, but their primary concern was the old principle of reserving the public lands for settlers.[20]

The repeal of the Southern Homestead Act passed the House of Representatives on June 7, with no new amendments. The vote was much closer than the one in the Senate. While 108 favored rescinding the law, 97 did not. Eighty-four did not vote.[21] Only one Republican, from South Carolina, approved of repeal. The four other representatives from the Palmetto State were all Republicans, and they voted with the rest of their party. The Democrats favored repeal by about 61 percent to 10 percent. But 30 percent of the Democrats did not vote.

The five southern public land states approved of revoking the act.

18. *Ibid.*, 3290–91; Gates, "Federal Land Policy in the South, 1866–1888," 310.
19. *Congressional Record*, 44th Cong., 1st Sess., 2461, 2603–2604.
20. *Ibid.*, 3292–93.
21. *Ibid.*, 3655. The figure for not voting as recorded in the *Record* is 83.

Fifteen voted yes, three voted no, and eight did not vote. The bill went to President Grant on June 22. He took no action, so it became law without his signature.[22]

Inquiries about repeal soon began to arrive at the General Land Office. Some simply asked for information; others wanted some points clarified. For example, could lands be homesteaded before they were offered at public sale? The commissioner stressed that the repeal did not interfere in any way with the homestead laws; therefore, the lands could still be homesteaded before they were offered.[23]

This inquiry was typical in that it implied repeal of the entire Southern Homestead Act. That was not the case. The new law simply repealed the homesteading-only restriction of the 1866 act. To clarify matters and to acquaint the local officers with the law, Commissioner J. A. Williamson issued a circular on July 19 that contained the new legislation. It said:

> The passage of this act does not change the condition of said lands as regards their liability to entry under the homestead laws, but its immediate effect is to lay open the same to the operation of the pre-emption laws, while it permits also the location thereon of such scrip as may be lawfully located upon "unoffered" lands.
>
> The said act does not open the public lands in said States to ordinary private entry until after they shall be offered at public sale, but it provides that this shall be done "as soon as practicable from time to time, and according to the provisions of the existing law."[24]

Ten years and one day after Andrew Johnson signed the Southern

22. The breakdown is as follows: Alabama's two Republicans did not vote; the Democrats all voted yes. Mississippi's vote was strictly partisan: the Republicans opposed, the Democrats favored. Louisiana was the most curious. One Republican voted nay; the other was absent. Of the four Democrats, one voted yea, the other three did not vote. Arkansas had no Republicans, but the three Democrats all voted yes. The other member, a Conservative, did not vote. Florida's Republican congressman was absent, and the Democratic one voted yes.

23. J. M. Doubleday to Commissioner, July 19, 1876, in MLR, M–19304; Commissioner to R&R, Harrison, August 8, 1876, in Letters Sent.

24. "Circular to the United States Registers and Receivers in Alabama, Mississippi, Louisiana, Arkansas, and Florida," July 19, 1876, in GLO Circulars, Orders and Notices, 1845–1876, Box 4, RG 49.

Homestead Act, its most meaningful provision was repealed: no longer were the southern public lands restricted to homesteading only. They were now subject to the same land laws as lands in the rest of the country. The circle had come complete. By 1876, the questions of Reconstruction were no longer crucial. As Paul Gates points out, "The southern land question had ceased to be confused with reconstruction issues and had become a problem in land economics and business policy."[25]

When it became law in 1866, the Southern Homestead Act embodied the free land, free labor ideology of the Republican party. Beyond that, though, its birth during the "critical year" connected the homestead principle irrevocably to Reconstruction. George W. Julian linked his antislavery, antisouthern views with land matters to produce a moderate measure to provide land to the landless, but more important, to punish the South. That the latter was his intention is obvious from his comments during the debate. That the measure was able to pass was due in no small part to the absence of the southern delegation in Congress. The act promised black landownership, and white southerners opposed it, not necessarily out of principle, but because they were terrified that the legislation would drain their labor supply. Southern landowners, therefore, saw the law as punitive, too. That might have been one reason Andrew Johnson signed it. Aside from being one of the earliest and most vocal advocates of the homestead principle, he wanted to punish large planters, who, he and radicals like Julian believed, had caused the war.

To say all of these things is to underscore the point that the law's architects and supporters were more interested in revenge than in creating an egalitarian society in the South. That is, their stress was on the antiplanter sentiment of the Republican party, not the egalitarian concern. As time went on, this lack of commitment to equality would emerge in the form of Republican-Conservative cooperation, with the goal of a return to prosperity. Republicans with

25. Gates, "Federal Land Policy," 311.

capital could woo former southern Whigs who had become Democrats by stressing the good news of prosperity and by downplaying the commitment to civil rights.

The failure of the Southern Homestead Act can be laid on different doorsteps. The execution of the law by the GLO and its local officers was the first problem. For one, the General Land Office was one of the most overburdened and bureaucratic agencies of its day; it was out of touch with the realities in the localities it governed. No guiding principle ever informed its policy decisions. When homesteaders proved that legislative enactments and agency decisions were practically useless, the GLO altered its policies to reflect existing needs. Ad hoc decisions add up to ad hoc policy. The result was close to chaos.

The GLO did not yet comprehend fully the meaning of land classification. Time and time again, homesteaders reminded Washington that not all the lands in the southern states were suitable for agriculture. Though the Southern Homestead Act assumed that land unsuitable for agriculture was worthless, timber interests proved this assumption groundless; the lands were extremely valuable for the timber on them.

The serious problems in executing the law on the local level contributed greatly to the failure of the act. Most, if not all, the registers and receivers were political appointments, and most of them demonstrated no great aptitude or concern for the land office business. The General Land Office's reprimands, the complaints against the officers filed by homesteaders, the faulty actions of the officers themselves, all added up to a less-than-desirable framework for the execution of the law. Aside from ignorance of the business or the laws, many of the appointees were southerners, some former Confederates, but mostly Union men. They often demonstrated antiblack attitudes.

The corruption and fraud accompanying the actions of the land officers almost always affected a homesteader's claim. Some officers were not above exacting exorbitant fees; others were willing to make deals with richer residents of the county to keep some unwanted types out. Some collected money for information and then never delivered the product. Others held the office as a sinecure and were never seen again. Many made deals or knowingly allowed illegal entries in order to skirt homesteading-only provisions.

If an officer took an active interest in helping persons locate homesteads and was above reproach, he was often frustrated by the poor condition of the land office records. Homesteaders repeatedly discovered, usually too late, that the tract books were inaccurate, that survey lines had been obliterated, that records had been destroyed. Usually settlers lost their improvements and their plots.

The status of the offices themselves presented problems. A land office might be closed for an extended period, or one office might be expected to serve a whole state or a large portion of a state. One of the constant complaints of homesteaders was the distance to the local office. Inconveniences caused by local officers and offices were by far the greatest problems encountered in trying to obtain land.

A second problem was the hostility to black landownership. Local officers blatantly discriminated against black applicants. Freedmen's Bureau officers, charged by O. O. Howard with affirmatively helping blacks locate public land, were often negligent, unconcerned, or more sympathetic to their white, former Confederate neighbors. The former rebels either did not want black neighbors or preferred to have them work out some arrangement to continue laboring on their old plantations.

Also, the philosophy of the age militated against the poor keeping land. Congress and the rhetoricians did not understand that it took capital and know-how to be a successful homesteader. The homestead principle assumed that anyone who wanted to homestead could successfully do it. This way of thinking ignored a great deal, namely, everything that came between the desire for a home and obtaining a final title. Homesteaders proved over and over again, by their words and their actions, that a five-year residency requirement meant nothing but catastrophe. The compulsory time spent on an uncleared tract meant no outside income or crops while the settler was trying to make his tract productive. In short, it was impossible to live. This was the era of individualism, hard work, and laissez-faire, and this philosophy was enshrined in the Southern Homestead Act. However, the fact is that it ignored those who began with nothing; that is to say, the philosophy of the age disregarded the hardships and the realities that most homesteaders faced.

Congress shared that philosophy. These people were ignorant of land quality. They were idealistic in the racial assumptions concerning treatment of blacks and black landownership in the South. They never followed through to see if their policies worked. They underestimated the powers of competitive capitalism. The Southern Homestead Act was a moderate measure, suited to political and economic exigencies of the time, but not to the realities. And here we touch on the root of the problem. Blaming the GLO and its officers, blaming prejudice and racial discrimination, blaming the naïveté of trying to begin anew with no help are all major concerns, but in the end, the context of Reconstruction politics ultimately doomed the Southern Homestead Act. Republicans at every level were more committed to their political success than to equality, and the history of the Southern Homestead Act, from its formulations to its repeal, speaks loudly of the nature of Reconstruction politics. It is no coincidence that repeal of the act came at the end of Reconstruction. The program failed because the act was only a mere gesture in the right direction.

APPENDIX A

Sampling Mississippi Homesteaders

The Federal Records Center at Suitland, Maryland, houses the homestead papers. These include the applications, affidavits, receipts, final proof papers, and final certificates. Taken together, these documents are at once a statistician's dream and a potential nightmare.

In order to assess the status and judge the utility of the available data bases, it was necessary to do pilot work on a relatively small random sample. This preliminary work would show several things: overall completeness of the data bases, completeness of individual records, labor intensity required to coordinate the information from the various records, and the ultimate utility of putting a great deal of work into data collection from these sources. I decided to select the random sample in a way that would provide some clues and insights into the southern homesteader. I chose to focus the pilot survey on Mississippi, primarily because it was the only southern state with one land office, and any random sample would reflect patterns throughout the entire state. What follows is a step-by-step account of my method and some warnings about interpreting the data and drawing conclusions.

Mississippi had a total of 8,797 original homestead applications during the period when the Southern Homestead Act was in effect. As in other states, the homestead papers are divided into two parts—applications that were canceled and applications that were patented. To make my sample as large as possible, I decided to sample as much from each category in the time I had—about one week. I allocated half of my time to canceled applications and half to patented applications. Using a table of random numbers, I first sampled from the canceled boxes. This produced a sample of 356 names or 5.6 percent of the total number of canceled applications (6,415). From the patented boxes, I sampled 284 names or 11.9 percent of the total number of patented applications (2,382). Canceled applications are filed by application number. However, patented applications were in the file by final certificate number. For the canceled entries, I randomly sampled from the application numbers; for the patented entries, I randomly sampled from the final certificate numbers. For all entries, I recorded the name, application number, township and range (location), the application date, and the acreage. For patented claims, the patent date was also noted. A note concerning the sample: if the randomly selected patent's application was past June 30, 1876, it was disregarded. Patenting took from five to seven years; therefore, the date of application had to be checked before the application could become part of the random sample.

Since race identification was not available on homestead applications, I needed to refer to the census, and since census data are arranged by county, I first had to locate each homestead on a map of the state to determine the county in which it was located. The initial operation was to sort all the homesteaders into counties for the purpose of consulting the census to ascertain race, age, and sex, if need be. I wrote librarians in Mississippi to find out if they had access to indexes of the 1870 and 1880 censuses. A few replied by actually doing the research for me, and I am grateful to them for shortening my task.

Approaching the census for this kind of work proved to be a more-than-frustrating job. The work ahead was staggering—locating 640 names in microfilmed manuscript censuses that are over one hundred years old. The federal government has indexed censuses dating back to 1880 by the sounds in the last name (the Soundex system). The 1880 census, of course, was taken after the Southern Homestead Act had been repealed. However, it was a start, so I devised a method for checking the census. County by county, I encoded the names according to the Soundex formulas and then consulted the 1880 census. Many names were there, but not all, not even half. There were reasons to expect this level of success; for instance, one rule was that only those families who had children at least ten years of age were recorded in the index.

If I could not locate the names, I then checked the 1870 rolls. One has to look carefully and concentrate intensely, because the process means turning from page to page while keeping in mind anywhere from one to about forty names. Census takers usually went door to door, certainly not in alphabetical order.

After I completed this tedious process, I entered this remaining data into the computer. Persons designated as mulatto were entered as "black" in my sample. Proofreading the output turned up several errors, which I corrected. The material was now ready for analysis. I worked with Dr. Donald Gantz, a statistician at George Mason University.

We quickly learned that one could not make far-reaching conclusions based on the available data. The explanation was simple: a large percentage of the homesteaders in the sample could not be found in the census. Among the reasons for the missing census data were the fact that people had moved, they were not recorded, they were recorded incorrectly, or I had simply missed them in the census. Of the 356 names in the sample of canceled applications, I located only 187 of them, or 52.5 percent. As one might expect, I had better luck with the successful, or patented, sample. But even there, I found 182, or only 64 percent, of the sample. This incomplete information makes drawing conclusions concerning race and age most difficult. Too many unknown variables mean assessments are not only tentative, but tenuous. Missing data are a statistician's worst enemy.

The computations in Tables 6 through 21 are based on known data only; therefore, they might not be representative of the total population. I would argue, however, this data can suggest useful, tentative patterns. The results are known as straightforward estimates and assume that applicants where information is *not* known are just like those where the information *is* known.

Tables 6 and 7 show the numbers of patented and canceled homesteads by race. It is important to note that they are displayed separately, since I sampled independently from each population. The sampling density was 5.6 percent of canceled entries and 11.9 percent of patented ones. The figures are calculated solely from the race-identified (*i.e.*, complete) data. The actual number for each race is divided by the total number of race-identified persons in the sample. Two persons identified as Indian are omitted here because they are statistically insignificant.

From these sample percentages, we can arrive at estimated figures for the total population. There were 6,415 cancellations and 2,382 patents for a total of 8,797 applications. By multiplying these known population totals by the percentages from the sample, we get an estimated breakdown by race and success of all applicants. The results are in Tables 8 and 9.

TABLE 6
Race Breakdown of Sample of Unsuccessful Applicants

Race	*Frequency*	*Percent*
Black	38	20.43
White	148	79.57
	186	100.00

TABLE 7
Race Breakdown of Sample of Successful Applicants

Race	*Frequency*	*Percent*
Black	53	29.28
White	128	70.72
	181	100.00

TABLE 8
Race Breakdown Estimates for All Unsuccessful Applicants

Race	*Frequency*
Black	1,311
White	5,104
	6,415

TABLE 9
Race Breakdown Estimates for All Successful Applicants

Race	*Frequency*
Black	697
White	1,685
	2,382

Table 10 combines the estimates of unsuccessful and successful applicants to give estimates of the total number of applicants classified by race.

TABLE 10
Estimates of All Applicants by Race

Race	*Frequency*	*Percent*
Black	2,008	22.83
White	6,789	77.17
	8,797	100.00

Now we can combine estimates to give us the calculated success ratios for each group. I divide the estimated number of successful black applicants (Table 9) by the estimated total number of black applicants (Table 10) to measure the black success rate. The same procedure applies for white applicants. The results are in Table 11.

TABLE 11
Success Rates by Race

Race	*Percent*
Black	34.71
White	24.82

Similar calculations can be performed with the data on sex. More information is available in this case, since sex can be most often determined by a person's name, even if that name did not appear in the census. If there was some doubt about sex or if the applicant put down his or her initials only, I recorded the data as unknown for that applicant. Of the 356 cancellations, I could identify 337 of them, or 94.66 percent. Of the 284 patented applications, I identified 269 or 94.71 percent.

Tables 12 and 13 show the actual sample percentages of unsuccessful and successful applicants by sex. I arrived at the figure by dividing the actual number of each group in the sample by the total number of both groups in the sample.

TABLE 12
Sex Breakdown of Sample of Unsuccessful Applicants

Sex	*Frequency*	*Percent*
Female	49	14.54
Male	288	85.46
	337	100.00

TABLE 13
Sex Breakdown of Sample of Successful Applicants

Sex	*Frequency*	*Percent*
Female	18	6.69
Male	251	93.31
	269	100.00

We can now determine estimates for the total population by multiplying the totals in each category by the percentages from the above tables. The results are in Tables 14 and 15.

TABLE 14
Sex Breakdown Estimates for All Unsuccessful Applicants

Sex	Frequency
Female	933
Male	5,482
	6,415

TABLE 15
Sex Breakdown Estimates for All Successful Applicants

Sex	Frequency
Female	159
Male	2,223
	2,382

Using the data from Tables 14 and 15, we now calculate the sex breakdown of all applicants. Simply add together the estimates of total numbers of unsuccessful and successful applicants (Table 16).

TABLE 16
Estimates of All Applicants by Sex

Sex	Frequency	Percent
Female	1,092	12.41
Male	7,705	87.59
	8,797	100.00

We can now combine these totals to give us the estimated success ratios for each group. Divide the estimated numbers of successful females and males by their total numbers, respectively (Table 17).

TABLE 17
Success Rates by Sex

Sex	Percent
Female	14.56
Male	28.85

With few exceptions, the census was also the source for age data, so there are problems of incomplete data similar to those for race. We ignore what we hope to be a minor problem in the analysis: that recorded ages may be inaccurate. The age used in the data set is the age of the homesteader at the time of application. The figure could be off one year, since the date of birth is not known. Of the total of 640 names, I located 392 of them, either in the census or recorded on the application papers. Table 18 presents an age breakdown of the sample.

TABLE 18
Age Statistics for Combined Samples of Unsuccessful and Successful Applicants

Number	392
Mean	37
Highest	72
Lowest	19
Median	34
75 Percentile	45*
24 Percentile	27*

*THE last two figures show the general range within which the middle 50 percent of ages fall.

We identified by race 362 of the 392 age-identified applicants. Age statistics for these 362 applicants, broken down by race, are presented in Table 19.

TABLE 19
Age Statistics Classified by Race

	Black	*White*
Number	87	274
Mean	39	36
Highest	66	72
Lowest	19	19
Median	36	33
75 Percentile	48	45
25 Percentile	30	25

The most complete and accurate data are the acreage figures, since the size of the homestead is known for all 640 applicants in the sample. A breakdown of the sample of all applicants is presented in Table 20.

TABLE 20
Acreage Statistics for Combined Samples of Unsuccessful and Successful Applicants

	All (640)	*Black (91)*	*White (276)*
Mean	91.70	97.20	96.36
Highest	180.32	165.64	180.32
Lowest	34.03	38.71	36.14
Median	80.10	80.30	80.28
75 Percentile	120.68	157.92	156.93
25 Percentile	73.14	79.62	79.41

Conclusions based on these data must be regarded as extremely tentative because the data are largely incomplete. The estimates derived in the tables above are true only if the population of unknowns reflects the one that is known; that is, these are straightforward estimates.

It is possible to take these unknowns into account statistically by creating "what if" scenarios or worst/best cases. These provide bounds on the true picture; however, this method usually stretches reality across too broad a range of possibilities. These boundaries can be figured on all the variables (race, sex, and age), but the race cases are the most intriguing.

The object of this exercise is to assign fractions of the unknowns to each race category. The best way to set boundaries is to use the extreme estimates. We can assume that all the unknowns are black, or that all the unknowns are white. That means 100 percent of the unknowns are black and none is white (best-case scenario), or 100 percent of the unknowns are white and none is black (worst-case scenario). The sample provides the following values:

TABLE 21
Race Breakdown of Sample of All Applicants

Race	*Successful*	*Unsuccessful*
Black	53	38
White	128	148
Unknown	102	169
	283	355

In the best-case scenario, where all the unknowns are black, there were 155 blacks out of 283 successful applicants, or 54.77 percent. Multiply that percentage by the total number of successful applicants (2,382) and the estimated number of black patents is 1,305. In this best-case scenario, there are no unsuccessful black homesteaders. That is to say, only 38, or 10.70 percent, of the 355 unsuccessful homesteaders were black. By multiplying that percentage by the 6,415 cancellations, one can estimate there were 686 unsuccessful black homesteaders. The total number of black applicants, then, is 1,991. Divide the estimate of black successes (1,305) by the estimate of the total number of black applicants (1,991) for a black success rate of 65.54 percent.

On the other extreme, all the unknown successful applicants are white, and all the unsuccessful unknowns are black. Using the same methods employed in the best-case scenario, one finds only 446 successful black applicants. On the other hand, there are 3,741 unsuccessful black applicants, for a total of 4,187 black applicants. In the worst-case scenario, then, the black success rate is approximately 10.65 percent.

The best-case scenario (1,991) means that blacks were 22.6 percent of all applicants (8,797). The worst-case scenario (4,187) makes blacks 47.60 percent of all applicants. This last high proportion underscores the absurdity of this extreme.

One final note for comparative purposes. One could assume that all the unknowns, both successful and unsuccessful, were white. This case provides the smallest percentage of black applicants, approximately 12.73 percent, with a success rate of 39.82 percent. The absurdity of the opposite scenario (that all the unknowns were black) precludes its consideration.

APPENDIX B

The Homesteads

TABLE 22
Original Homestead Applications

State	*1867*[a]	*1868*	*1869*	*1870*	*1871*
Alabama	616	1,646	2,192	2,565	1,388
Arkansas	835	2,830	2,214	4,596	4,571
Florida	1,505	1,781	744	678	217
Louisiana	259	0	582	711	1,023
Mississippi	555	1,602	935	1,109	882
Total	3,770	7,859	6,667	9,659	8,081

TABLE 23
Acreage of Original Homestead Applications

State	*1867*	*1868*	*1869*	*1870*	*1871*
Alabama	47,224.9	124,085.2	209,004.4	243,833.3	129,301.0
Arkansas	50,418.7	183,232.4	196,418.9	431,797.5	367,021.7
Florida	111,878.2	115,935.8	75,269.5	69,778.1	24,969.6
Louisiana	20,164.6	0	63,003.2	90,101.5	133,430.6
Mississippi	31,427.8	102,824.5	78,809.5	100,806.5	71,177.2
Total	261,114.2	526,077.9	622,505.5	936,316.9	725,900.1

1872	1873	1874	1875	1876	Total
1,647	1,653	1,742	1,260	1,575	16,284
3,716	2,497	2,308	1,235	1,593	26,395
697	359	689	956	2,049	9,675
1,194	1,202	381	474	626	6,452
1,375	841	548	410	540	8,797
8,629	6,552	5,668	4,335	6,383	67,603

SOURCE: Thomas Donaldson, *The Public Domain* (Washington, D.C., 1884), 352–54.
[a]The fiscal year ran from July 1 to June 30.

1872	1873	1874	1875	1876	Total
162,762.4	167,763.6	181,730.7	123,238.9	157,624.6	1,546,569.0
366,623.2	246,253.5	239,226.8	128,230.5	158,666.7	2,367,889.9
80,783.2	41,136.2	80,521.7	115,430.5	252,492.6	968,195.4
142,172.9	137,363.7	44,957.6	50,104.2	66,983.4	748,281.7
146,700.7	87,380.0	52,151.6	36,702.0	50,481.1	758,460.9
899,042.4	679,897.0	598,588.4	453,706.1	686,248.4	6,389,396.9

SOURCE: Thomas Donaldson, *The Public Domain* (Washington, D.C., 1884), 352–54.

TABLE 24
Final Proof

State	1871	1872	1873	1874	1875	1876	1877
Alabama		20	62	150	442	906	610
Arkansas	11	72	211	828	1,344	1,963	1,735
Florida		23	32	443	336	273	171
Louisiana		9	5	38	177	256	352
Mississippi		9	162	162	162	211	192
Total	11	133	472	1,621	2,461	3,609	3,060

TABLE 25
Final Proof Average

State	1871	1872	1873	1874	1875	1876	1877
Alabama		1,564.9	4,593.7	13,177.7	43,735.2	99,292.2	59,540.6
Arkansas	824.6	3,947.1	14,746.7	68,655.1	122,299.5	188,617.5	177,853.5
Florida		1,288.1	2,136.7	32,053.1	31,661.0	28,387.8	17,693.8
Louisiana		703.1	402.3	3,872.5	21,093.9	30,355.7	43,432.0
Mississippi		538.6	8,590.6	12,123.2	13,706.7	20,002.5	20,466.8
Total	824.6	8,041.8	30,470.0	129,881.6	232,496.3	366,655.7	318,986.7

1878	*1879*	*1880*	*1881*	*1882*	*1883*	*Total*
584	544	399	626	884	1,066	6,293
1,808	987	986	862	755	1,118	12,680
216	214	271	564	762	767	4,072
406	334	197	227	187	185	2,373
386	309	95	227	179	288	2,382
3,400	2,388	1,948	2,506	2,767	3,424	27,800

SOURCE: Thomas Donaldson, *The Public Domain* (Washington, D.C., 1884), 352–54, 1016, 1284.

1878	*1879*	*1880*	*1881*	*1882*	*1883*	*Total*
60,077.9	55,609.0	43,834.2	63,826.4	96,896.1	178,625.4	720,773.3
185,030.3	103,675.3	110,195.1	89,534.6	77,243.8	117,023.7	1,259,646.8
23,856.3	22,583.7	33,043.0	69,272.8	91,726.7	90,201.4	443,904.4
51,339.5	41,045.6	25,280.0	26,470.4	20,737.2	20,996.9	285,729.1
40,193.3	35,709.5	10,768.9	22,702.9	18,627.9	32,603.8	236,034.7
360,497.3	258,623.1	223,121.2	271,807.1	305,231.7	439,451.2	2,946,088.3

SOURCE: Thomas Donaldson, *The Public Domain* (Washington, D.C., 1884), 352–54, 1016, 1284.

Bibliography

Primary Sources

Articles and Books

Boyd, Julian, ed. *The Papers of Thomas Jefferson.* Vol. I of 20 vols. Princeton, 1950.

Carrigan, Alfred Holt. "Reminiscences of the Secession Convention." Arkansas Historical Association Publications, I (1906), 305–13.

Donaldson, Thomas C. *The Public Domain: Its History with Statistics, to June 30 and December 1, 1883.* Washington, D.C., 1884.

Graf, Leroy P., and Ralph W. Haskins, eds. *The Papers of Andrew Johnson.* 7 vols. Knoxville, 1967–86.

Israel, Fred L., ed. *The State of the Union Messages of the Presidents 1790–1966.* Vol. I of 3 vols. New York, 1966.

Julian, G. W. "Our Land Policy." *Atlantic Monthly,* XLIII (March, 1879), 325–37.

———. *Political Recollections 1840 to 1872.* Chicago, 1884.

———. *Speeches on Political Questions.* Cambridge, Mass., 1872.

McPherson, Edward. *A Handbook of Politics for 1868.* Washington, D.C., 1868.

Government Documents

A Bill for the Disposal of the Public Lands for Homestead Actual Settlement in the States of Alabama, Mississippi, Louisiana, Arkansas, and Florida. H.R. 85, 39th Cong., 1st Sess.

A Bill to Declare Forfeited to the United States Certain Lands Granted to Aid in the Construction of Railroads in the States of Alabama, Mississippi, Louisiana, and Florida, and for other Purposes H.R. 267, 40th Cong., 2nd Sess.

A Bill to Facilitate the Occupation of Public Lands by Freedmen Under the Homestead Act. H.R. 122, 40th Cong., 1st Sess.
A Bill to Incorporate the Freedmen's Homestead Company. H.R. 2970, 41st Cong., 3rd Sess.
A Bill to Repeal Section Two Thousand Three Hundred and Three of the Revised Statutes of the United States, Making Restrictions in the Disposition of the Public Lands in the States of Alabama, Mississippi, Louisiana, Arkansas, and Florida. S. 2, 44th Cong., 1st Sess.
Congressional Globe, 30th Cong., 2nd Sess., to 42nd Cong., 3rd Sess.
Congressional Record, 43rd Cong., 1st Sess., to 44th Cong., 2nd Sess.
Freedmen's Bureau Act. Statutes at Large, Vol. XIV, Chap. 200.
Homestead Act. Statutes at Large. Vol. XII.
Homestead Act. Statutes at Large. Vol. XIII.
House Executive Documents. 34th Cong., 1st Sess., No. 13.
House Journal. 33rd Cong., 1st Sess.
House Journal. 36th Cong., 1st Sess.
House Journal. 39th Cong., 1st Sess.
House Reports. Condition of the South. 43rd Cong., 2nd Sess.
Senate Documents. Journal of the Congress of the Confederate States of America, 1861–1865. 58th Cong., 2nd Sess.
Senate Journal. 36th Cong., 1st Sess.
Senate Journal. 39th Cong., 1st Sess.
Soldiers' and Sailors' Homestead Act. Statutes at Large, Vol. XVII.
Southern Homestead Act. Statutes at Large, Vol. XIV.

Manuscripts

Library of Congress, Washington, D.C.
Blaine, James G. Papers.
Giddings, Joshua (George W. Julian). Papers.
Grant, U.S. Papers.
Johnson, Andrew. Papers.
Stevens, Thaddeus. Papers.
National Archives, Washington, D.C.
Freedmen's Bureau, Record Group 105.
Records of the Assistant Commissioner for the State of Louisiana, 1865–1869. Microfilm edition, M1027.
Registers and Letters Received by the Bureau of Refugees, Freedmen, and Abandoned Lands, 1865–1872. Microfilm edition, M752.
Selected Series of Records Issued by the Commissioner of the Bureau of Refugees, Freedmen and Abandoned Lands, 1865–1872. Microfilm edition, M742.

General Land Office, Record Group 49.
Bond Book. Field Officers. Vols. III–IV.
Cartographic Records. Land Offices and Districts and Officials.
Circulars, Orders, and Notices, 1845–1876. Box 4.
Circulars to State Land Officials. Vol. I (1821–72).
Circulars to State Land Officials, 1851–1880. Vols. II–III.
Division "A." Department and Congressional Letters Sent, September 7, 1871–July 18, 1876. 4 vols.
Division "A." Letters Sent Pertaining to Removal of Land Offices, 1866–76.
Division "A." Letters Sent to Registers and Receivers of Local Land Offices, October 24, 1871–October 25, 1876. 3 vols.
Division "C." Letters Sent to Members of Congress, April 1, 1868–December 1, 1876.
Division "C." Letters Sent to Other Government Departments, January 4, 1866–October 1, 1876. 8 vols.
Division "C." Letters Sent to Registers and Receivers, May 19, 1865–November 15, 1876.
Division "C." Miscellaneous Letters Sent by the General Land Office, 1796–1889. Microfilm edition, M25.
Division "D." Copies of Executive Orders Relating to Land Matters, 1863–93. Box 4.
Division "D." Miscellaneous Letters Received from Private Persons, Land Entrymen, Attorneys, and Other Persons, 1866–76.
Division "D." Original Executive Orders File, 1866–76. Boxes 4–7.
Division "D." Printed Copies of Proclamations of Presidents from 1859–1897.
Division "D." Registers of Letters Received from Members of Congress, 1865–76.
Division "D." Registers of Letters Received, June 1, 1867–December 31, 1876. Surveyors General. Vols. IX–XI.
Division "D." Registers of Miscellaneous Letters Received from Private Persons, Attorneys, and Entrymen, 1866–76.
Division "E." Congressional Letters Received. Box 25.
Division "E." Letters Received from Surveyors General, June 19, 1869–December 31, 1876. Florida.
Division "E." Letters Received from Surveyors General, July 20, 1869–December 23, 1876. Louisiana.
Division "E." Letters Sent to Surveyors General, May 9, 1865–December 28, 1876. All states. 10 vols.
Division "M." Record of the Disposal of Public Lands Under the Home-

stead Laws Approved May 20, 1862 and Acts Amendatory Thereof up to and Including the Fiscal Year. 1863–1912.
Division "N." Record Copies of General Letters Sent. Vol. III. (Mineral Contests.)
Land District Notices, October 29, 1870–May 29, 1889. Vol. I. Notices 745–924.
Office of the Secretary of the Interior, Record Group 48.
Appointments Division
Appointment Papers, U.S. Land Officers, Alabama, Arkansas, Florida, Louisiana, and Mississippi.
"Lists and Registers of Appointees and Employees," Compilation of Names and Appointees to General Land Office Field Positions, 1861–76.
Land and Railroads Division
Letters Received from the Commissioner of the General Land Office, January 31, 1866–November, 1876.
Letters Received from the Presidents, 1849–80.
Letters Sent, 1866–76.
Letters Sent to the Commissioner of the General Land Office, January 1866–July, 1872.
Registers of Letters Received from the Commissioner of the General Land Office, Vols. IV–VI (January 2, 1866–November, 1876).

Miscellaneous Government Documents

Department of Interior. General Land Office. *Annual Report of the Commissioner of the General Land Office,* 1866.
Department of Interior. General Land Office. *Annual Report of the Commissioner of the General Land Office,* 1932.
Register of Officers and Agents, Civil, Military, and Naval, in the Service of the United States. September, 1867–September, 1877. [Official Register.]

Newspapers

Boston *Daily Advertiser,* 1866, 1876.
Chicago *Tribune,* 1866, 1876.
Cincinnati *Daily Enquirer,* April 3, 1878.
Huntsville *Advocate,* November, 1865–August 8, 1866.
Jackson *Daily Mississippi Clarion and Standard,* 1866, 1876.
Little Rock *Daily Gazette,* 1866–76.
Memphis *Daily Commercial,* 1866.
Mobile *Daily Advertiser and Register,* 1866, 1876.
New Orleans *Republican,* 1876.

New Orleans *Times*, 1866, 1876.
New York *Herald*, 1866, 1876.
New York *Tribune*, 1866.
New York *World*, 1866, 1876.
Vicksburg *Daily Herald*, 1866.

Secondary Sources

Abbott, Martin. "Free Land, Free Labor, and the Freedmen's Bureau." *Agricultural History*, XXX (1956), 150–56.
Baumgardner, James L. "Andrew Johnson and the Patronage." Ph.D. dissertation, University of Tennessee, 1968.
Bentley, George R. *A History of the Freedmen's Bureau*. Philadelphia, 1955.
Bettersworth, John K. *Confederate Mississippi*. 1943; rpr. Philadelphia, 1978.
Biographical Directory of the American Congress. Washington, D.C., 1971.
Clawson, Marion. *The Bureau of Land Management*. New York, 1971.
———. *Uncle Sam's Acres*. Westport, Conn., 1970.
Clawson, Marion, and Burnell Held. *The Federal Lands: Their Use and Management*. Baltimore, 1957.
Conover, Milton. *The General Land Office: Its History, Activities, and Organization*. Baltimore, 1923.
Cox, John H., and LaWanda Cox. *Politics, Principle, and Prejudice 1865–1866: Dilemma of Reconstruction America*. Glencoe, N.Y., 1963.
———, eds. *Reconstruction, the Negro, and the New South*. New York, 1973.
Cox, LaWanda. "The Promise of Land for the Freedmen." *Mississippi Valley Historical Review*, XLV (1958), 413–40.
Cruden, Robert. *The Negro in Reconstruction*. Englewood Cliffs, N.J., 1969.
Donald, David Herbert. *The Politics of Reconstruction*. Baton Rouge, 1965.
Dougan, Michael B. *Confederate Arkansas: The People and Policies of a Frontier State in Wartime*. University, Ala., 1976.
Du Bois, W. E. B. *Black Reconstruction*. New York, 1935.
Dunham, Harold Hathaway. "Government Handout: A Study in the Administration of the Public Lands 1875–1891." Ph.D. dissertation, Columbia University, 1941.
Fleming, Walter L. *Civil War and Reconstruction in Alabama*. 1905; rpr. Gloucester, Mass., 1949.
Foner, Eric. *Free Soil, Free Labor, Free Men: The Ideology of the Republican Party Before the Civil War*. New York, 1970.
———. *Nothing But Freedom: Emancipation and Its Legacy*. Baton Rouge, 1983.

———. *Politics and Ideology in the Age of the Civil War.* New York, 1980.
———. *Reconstruction, 1863–1877.* New York, 1988.
Franklin, John Hope. "Mirror for Americans: A Century of Reconstruction History." *American Historical Review,* LXXXV (1980), 1–14.
———. *Reconstruction After the Civil War.* Chicago, 1967.
Gates, Paul W. *Agriculture and the Civil War.* New York, 1965.
———. "Federal Land Policy in the South, 1866–1888." *Journal of Southern History,* VI (1940), 303–30.
———. *History of the Public Land Law Development.* Washington, D.C., 1969.
———. "The Homestead Law in an Incongruous Land System." *American Historical Review,* XLI (1936), 652–81.
Harris, William C. *The Day of the Carpetbagger: Republican Reconstruction in Mississippi.* Baton Rouge, 1979.
Hermann, Janet Sharp. *The Pursuit of a Dream.* New York, 1981.
Hibbard, Benjamin H. *A History of the Public Land Policies.* 1924; rpr. Madison, 1965.
Hoffnagle, Warren. "The Southern Homestead Act: Its Origins and Operation." *Historian,* XXXII (1970), 612–29.
Johns, John E. *Florida During the Civil War.* Gainesville, 1963.
Kolchin, Peter R. *First Freedom: The Responses of Alabama Blacks to Emancipation and Reconstruction.* Westport, Conn., 1972.
Litwack, Leon F. *Been in the Storm So Long: The Aftermath of Slavery.* New York, 1979.
McFeely, William S. *Grant: A Biography.* New York, 1981.
McKitrick, Eric L. *Andrew Johnson and Reconstruction.* Chicago, 1964.
Magdol, Edward. *A Right to the Land: Essays on the Freedmen's Community.* Westport, Conn., 1977.
Mandle, Jay R. *The Roots of Black Poverty: The Southern Plantation Economy after the Civil War.* Durham, 1978.
Oubre, Claude F. *Forty Acres and a Mule.* Baton Rouge, 1978.
———. "'Forty Acres and a Mule': Louisiana and the Southern Homestead Act." *Louisiana History,* XVII (1976), 143–57.
———. "The Freedmen's Bureau and Negro Land Ownership." M.A. thesis, University of Southwestern Louisiana, 1970.
Perman, Michael. *Emancipation and Reconstruction, 1862–1879.* Arlington Heights, Ill., 1987.
———. *Reunion Without Compromise: The South and Reconstruction, 1865–1868.* Cambridge, England, 1973.
———. *The Road to Redemption: Southern Politics, 1869–1879.* Chapel Hill, 1984.

Pope, Christine Farnham. "The Southern Homestead Act: A Punitive Measure." M.A. thesis, University of Chicago, 1962.
———. "Southern Homesteads for Negroes." *Agricultural History,* XLIV (1970), 201–12.
Rabinowitz, Howard N. "Holland Thompson and Black Political Participation in Montgomery, Alabama." In *Southern Black Leaders of the Reconstruction Era,* edited by Howard N. Rabinowitz. Urbana, 1982.
Richardson, Joe M. *The Negro in the Reconstruction of Florida, 1865–1877.* Tallahassee, 1965.
Riddleberger, Patrick W. "George W. Julian: Abolitionist Land Reformer." *Agricultural History,* XXIX (1955), 108–15.
———. "The Making of a Political Abolitionist: George W. Julian and the Free Soilers, 1848." *Indiana Magazine of History,* LI (1955), 221–36.
———. "The Radicals' Abandonment of the Negro during Reconstruction." *Journal of Negro History,* XLIV (1960), 88–102.
Ringold, May Spencer. *The Role of the State Legislatures in the Confederacy.* Athens, Ga., 1966.
Robbins, Roy M. *Our Landed Heritage: The Public Domain, 1776–1936.* Princeton, 1942.
———. "The Public Domain in the Era of Exploitation, 1862–1901." *Agricultural History,* XIII (1939), 97–108.
Rohrbough, Malcolm J. *The Land Office Business: The Settlement and Administration of American Public Lands, 1789–1837.* New York, 1968.
Rose, Willie Lee. *Rehearsal for Reconstruction: The Port Royal Experiment.* London, 1964.
Saloutos, Theodore. "Southern Agriculture and the Problems of Readjustment: 1865–1877." *Agricultural History,* XXX (1956), 58–76.
Shofner, Jerrell H. *Nor Is It Over Yet: Florida in the Era of Reconstruction, 1863–1877.* Gainesville, 1974.
Smith, Henry Nash. *Virgin Land: The American West as Symbol and Myth.* New York, 1950.
Stampp, Kenneth M. *Era of Reconstruction.* New York, 1966.
Summers, Mark W. *Railroads, Reconstruction, and the Gospel of Prosperity: Aid Under the Radical Republicans, 1865–1877.* Princeton, 1984.
Taylor, Joe Gray. *Louisiana Reconstructed, 1863–1877.* Baton Rouge, 1974.
Wharton, Vernon L. *The Negro in Mississippi, 1865–1890.* New York, 1965.
Wiener, Jonathan M. *Social Origins of the New South: Alabama, 1860–1885.* Baton Rouge, 1978.
Wiggins, Sarah Woolfolk. *The Scalawag in Alabama Politics, 1865–1881.* University, Ala., 1977.

Wood, Gordon. *The Creation of the American Republic, 1776–1787*. Chapel Hill, 1969.

Woodward, C. Vann. *Origins of the New South, 1877–1913*. Baton Rouge, 1951.

Zeichner, Oscar. "The Transition from Slave to Free Agricultural Labor in the Southern States." *Agricultural History*, XIII (1939), 22–32.

Index